Macroeconomics

Revision Guide for the Introductory Economics Student

Appropriate for the following courses:

Advanced Placement Macroeconomics
International Baccalaureate Economics, Higher and Standard Level
A Level Economics
Introduction to Microeconomics at the university level

JASON WELKER

www.welkerswikinomics.com

ISBN: 1482612178
ISBN-13: 978-1482612172

DEDICATION

For Libby

CONTENTS

Introduction to the Series

Thank you for purchasing the Welker's Wikinomics Macroeconomics and International Economics Revision Guide. This book is just one of many resources available from Welker's Wikinomics, a website created in 2007 to provide Economics students and teachers with resources to help them learn Economics in an easy and enjoyable manner.

Jason Welker teaches International Baccalaureate and Advanced Placement Economics at Zurich International School in Switzerland, where he has lived with his wife since 2008 (and as of 2012, his new daughter). Prior to teaching in Zurich, Jason taught Economics at the Shanghai American School in China. Jason graduated from university with degrees in Economics and Education after spending his own high school years living and studying at an international school in Malaysia.

In addition to this book, Welker's Wikinomics also publishes a revision guide for Microeconomics appropriate for students in either the AP or IB Economics class (standard and higher level), or an introductory Macroeconomics course at the university level. The Microeconomics revision guide includes chapters on the following topics:

- Supply, Demand and Equilibrium
- Elasticities
- Government Intervention in Markets
- Market Failure
- Costs of Production
- Perfect Competition

- Pure Monopoly
- Monopolistic Competition and Oligopoly
- Theory of Consumer Behavior
- Resource Markets
- Microeconomics Glossary

Many more resources are available for free from Welker's Wikinomics online. These include:

- PowerPoint's for Economics teachers covering every unit from an introductory course: www.welkerswikinomics.com/lecturenotes
- A blog that is regularly updated with news and analysis appropriate for introductory economics students: www.economicsinplainenglish.com
- Video lectures covering nearly every topic in both this revision guide and the Macroeconomic guide: www.econclassroom.com
- A mobile application providing access to all the resources from the above sites, available for both Android and Apple devices: www.econclassroom.conduitapps.com
- A variety of other resources to aid the Economics student and teacher in mastering the subject available at www.welkerswikinomics.com

As you use this guide to review, you will notice that at the top of each page there is a reference to a section from the Economics Classroom website. For example, in chapter 3, the top of each page says "www.EconClassroom.com – 2.2" By going to section 2.2 of the website, you will find video lessons relating to Aggregate Demand and Aggregate Supply.

These are here to remind you, the student, that most topics from this book are presented in video lectures by Jason at his website, www.econclassroom.com. This site is organized by sections of the syllabus, which in turn correspond with chapters from this book. The most effective way to use this book, therefore, is in conjunction with the video lectures and other resources available online.

Chapter 1 – Introduction to Economics

Economics as a Social Science

- Explain that Economics is a social science
- Outline the social scientific method.
- Explain the process of model building in economics.
- Explain that economists must use the *ceteris paribus* assumption when developing economic models.
- Distinguish between positive and normative economics.
- Examine the assumption of rational economic decision-making

Scarcity

- Explain that scarcity exists because factors of production are finite and wants are infinite
- Explain that economics studies the ways in which resources are allocated to meet needs and wants
- Explain that the three basic economic questions that must be answered by any economic system are: "What to produce?", "How to produce?" and "For whom to produce?"

Choice and Opportunity Cost

- Explain that as a result of scarcity, choices have to be made
- Explain that when an economic choice is made, an alternative is always foregone
- Explain that a production possibilities curve (production possibilities frontier) model may be used to show the concepts of scarcity, choice, opportunity cost and a situation of unemployed resources and inefficiency.

Central Themes

- The extent to which governments should intervene in the allocation of resources
- The threat to sustainability as a result of the current patterns of resource allocation
- The extent to which the goal of economic efficiency may conflict with the goal of equity
- The distinction between economic growth and economic development

Economics is a Social Science

Economics is the *social science* that studies the interactions of humans in the commercial realm. Economists examine the way societies allocate their *scarce resources* towards *competing wants and needs* and seek to develop systems that achieve certain objectives, including:

- Growth in humans' standard of living over time
- Sustainable development
- Employment and stability

Microeconomics vs. Macroeconomics

Economics is divided into two main fields of study

Microeconomics: Studies the behaviors of individuals within an economy, including consumers and producers in the market for particular goods. Examples of microeconomic topics:

- The Automobile market in Switzerland,
- the market for movie tickets in Seattle,
- the market for airline tickets between the US and Europe,
- the market for vacations to Spain,
- the market for international school teachers.

Macroeconomics: Studies the total effect on a nation's people of all the economic activity within that nation. The four main concerns of macroeconomics are:

- total output of a nation,
- the average price level of a nation,
- the level of employment (or unemployment) in the nation and
- the distribution of income in the nation
- Examples of macroeconomic topics: Unemployment in Canada, inflation in Zimbabwe, economic growth in China, the gap between the rich and the poor in America

Microeconomics and macroeconomics can be broken down into many smaller topics. Some of them are identified below.

Microeconomics topics	Macroeconomics topics
Individual markets	National markets
the behavior of firms (companies) and consumers	Total output and income of nations
the allocation of land, labor and capital resources	Total supply and demand of the nation
Supply and demand	Taxes and government spending
The efficiency of markets	Interest rates and central banks
Product markets	Unemployment and inflation
Supply and Demand	Income distribution
Profit maximization	Economics growth and development
Utility maximization	International trade
Competition	
Market failure	

Fundamental Concepts of Economics

Whether we study micro or macro, there are some basic concepts that underlie all fields of Economics study

Scarcity:	Economics is about the allocation of scarce resources among society's various needs and wants.
Resources:	Economics is about the allocation of resources among society's various needs and wants.
Tradeoffs:	Individuals and society as whole are constantly making choices involving tradeoffs between alternatives. Whether it's what goods to consume, what goods to produce, how to produce them, and so on.
Opportunity Cost:	"The opportunity cost is the opportunity lost". In other words, every economic decision involves giving up something. NOTHING IS FREE!!

Model Building in Economics

A popular tool in the Economist's kit is the *economic model*. Just like scientists in other fields, economists use models to represent something from the real world.

A model of the solar system: Allows astronomers to illustrate in a simplified model the relationships between solar bodies.

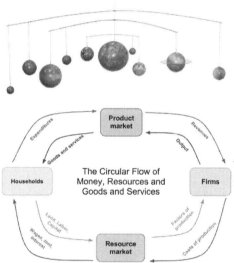

A Circular Flow Model: Allows economists to illustrate in a simplified model the relationships between households and firms in a market economy.

Ceteris Paribus: Like in other sciences, when using economic models we must assume "all else equal". This allows us to observe how one variable in an economy will affect another, without considering all the other factors that may affect the variable in question.

Positive and Normative Economics

Economists explore the world of facts and data, but also often draw conclusions or prescribe policies based more on interpretation or even their own opinions. It is important to distinguish at all times whether the focus of our studies is in the realm of *positive* or *normative* Economics

Positive economic statements: Each of the following statements is a statement of fact, and each can be supported by evidence based on quantifiable observations of the world.

- *Unemployment rose by 0.8 percent last quarter as 250,000 Americans lost their jobs in both the public and private sectors.*
- *Rising pork prices have led to a surge in demand for chicken across China.*

- *Increased use of public transportation reduces congestion on city streets and lowers traffic fatality rates.*

Normative economic statements: Each of the following statements is based on observable, quantifiable variables, but each includes an element of opinion

- *Unemployment rates are higher among less educated workers; therefore government should include education and job training programs as a component of benefits for the nation's unemployed.*
- *Rising pork prices harm low-income households whose incomes go primarily towards food, therefore, to slow the rise in food prices, the Chinese government should enforce a maximum price scheme on the nation's pork industry.*
- *It is the government's obligation to provide public transportation options to the nation's people to relieve the negative environmental and health effects of traffic congestion.*

Introduction to Scarcity

You may not know it yet, but you are beginning a science class. Yes, Economics is a science, and just like other sciences, it deals with a fundamental problem of nature.

- Think of Aerospace Engineering. This is a science that struggles to overcome a basic problem of nature, that of <u>GRAVITY</u>. Aerospace Engineers are scientists whose research and life's work is aimed at overcoming the problem of gravity and putting man in space.
- Economists are also scientists whose work attempts to overcome a basic problem of nature.

A riddle:

What is the basic problem of nature that the science of Economic attempts to overcome?

Hint: It arises because of the limited nature of earth's natural resources!

The answer: SCARCITY!

Scarcity is the *basic problem of Economics.*

Scarcity arises when something is both limited in quantity yet desired

Some facts about scarcity

- Not all goods are scarce, but most are
- Some goods that humans consume are infinite, such as air

Scarce (limited and desired)	**Not Scarce** (not limited OR not desired)
Diamonds, Apartments, Drinking water, Teachers, Doctors, Cars, Medical services	Air, Salt water, Mosquitos, Malaria, Love, HIV, Crime

So, what makes something scarce?

Here's another riddle for you…

- Nobody needs diamonds, yet they are extremely valuable
- Everybody needs water, yet they are extremely cheap

Why Are Diamonds So Expensive?
Why Is Water So Cheap?

This is known as the "diamond / water paradox". The answer lies in the fact that *economic value is derived from scarcity*

- *The more scarce an item, the more valuable it is*
- *The less scarce, the less value it has in society!*

Free Goods and Economics Goods

Goods in Economics are those things we like to consume. They are called "goods" because consuming them makes us feel good!

- Free goods are those things that we desire but that are not limited
- Economic goods are those that we desire but that ARE limited

Which of these goods are Free Goods and which are Economic Goods?					
Haircuts	Cars	Toothbrushes	Televisions	Movies	Happiness
Shoes	Vacations	Friendship	Hamburgers	Love	Jewelry
Education	Air	Fresh Water	Public Transportation	Sunshine	Rain

The Factors of Production

The production of all of the goods we desire requires scarce resources. It is the allocation of these resources between humans' competing wants that Economics focuses on.

Land	Labor	Capital	Entrepreneurship
Land resources are those things that are "gifts of nature". The soil in which we grow food, wood, minerals such as copper and tin and resources such as oil, goal, gas and uranium are scarce	Labor refers to the human resources used in the production of goods and services. Labor is the human work, both physical and intellectual, that contributes to the production of goods and services	Capital refers to the *tools and technologies* that are used to produce the goods and services we desire. Since more and better tools enhance the production of all types of goods and services, from cars to computers to education to haircuts, yet the amount of capital in the world is limited, *capital* is a scarce resource.	This refers to the innovation and creativity applied in the production of goods and services. The physical scarcity of land, labor and capital does not apply to human ingenuity, which itself is a resource that goes into the production of out economic output.

"The Basic Economic Problem"

In a world of finite resources, the wants of man are virtually infinite. The basic Economic Problem is how to allocate those limited, scarce resources between the unlimited wants of man. This problem gives rise to three questions that any and all economic systems must address. The Three Basic Economics Questions are:

1. *What should be produced?* Given the resources with which society is endowed, what combination of different goods and services should be produced?
2. *How should things be produced?* Should production use lots of labor, or should lots of capital and technology be used?
3. *Who should things be produced for?* How should the output that society produces be distributed? Should everyone keep what he or she makes, or should trade take place? Should everyone be given equal amounts of the output, or should it be every man for himself?

These are the three guiding questions of any Economic system

Free Trade

The market system allocates society's scarce resources through the free, voluntary exchanges of individuals, households and firms in the free market. These exchanges are broadly known as "trade". Trade can exist between individuals, or between entire nations. Trade between countries is called International Trade.

Trade is one of the concepts fundamental to the field of economics.

- Voluntary exchanges between individuals and firms in resource and product markets involving the exchange of goods, services, land, labor and capital represent a type of trade.
- International trade involves the exchange of resources, goods, services and assets (both real and financial) across national boundaries.
- Trade makes everyone better off, and leads to a more efficient allocation of society's scarce resources.

Opportunity Cost

Perhaps the most fundamental concept to Economics, opportunity cost is what must be given up in order to undertake any activity or economic exchange.

- Opportunity costs are not necessarily monetary; rather when you buy something the opportunity cost is what you *could have done* with the money you spent on that thing.
- Even non-monetary exchanges involve opportunity costs, as you may have done something different with the time you chose to spend undertaking any activity in your life.

Examples of opportunity costs

- The opportunity cost of watching TV on a weeknight is the benefit you could have gotten from studying.
- The opportunity cost of going to college is the income you could have earned by getting a job out of high school
- The opportunity cost of starting your own business in the wages you give up by working for another company
- The opportunity cost of using forest resources to build houses is the enjoyment people get from having pristine forests.

The Production Possibilities Model
- The tradeoff we face between the use of our scarce resources (or even time) can be modeled in a simple Economic graph known as the Production Possibilities Curve (the PPC). Study the graph below:

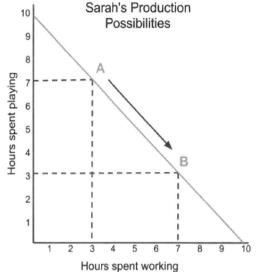

Tradeoffs in the PPC: Sarah faces two tradeoffs. She can either work or play with her limited amount of time.
- The opportunity cost of an hour of work is an hour of play
- As she goes from 3 hours of work to 7 hours of work, she gives up 4 hours of play.
- She cannot spend 10 hours working AND 10 hours playing, so Sarah has to make CHOICES

This basic model can be used to illustrate the economic challenges faced by individuals, firms, states, countries or the entire world…

Consider the hypothetical PPC for the country of Italy
This model shows that Italy can produce:
- Either 7.5 million pizzas,
- OR 750 robots
- Note, however, that Italy can NOT produce 7.5 million pizzas AND 750 robots

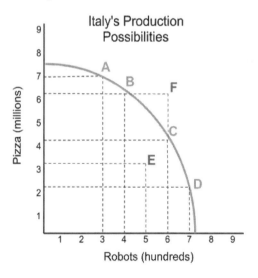

Italy faces a tradeoff in how to use its scarce resources of land, labor and capital. As the country moves along its PPC from point A to point D:
- It gives up more and more pizza to have more robots
- It gives up current consumption of food for production of robots, which themselves are capital goods, and therefore will assure that Italy's economy will grow into the future.

Assumptions about the PPC
1. A point ON the PPC is attainable only if a nation achieves full-employment of its productive resources
2. The nation's resources are fixed in quantity
3. The economy is closed, i.e. does not trade with other countries
4. Represents only one country's economy

Observations about points on or within the PPC
- Points ON the PPC are attainable, and desirable, since a country producing on the line is achieving full employment and efficiency
- Points inside the PPC (such as E) are attainable but undesirable, because a nation producing here has unemployment and is inefficient
- Points outside the PPC (such as F) are unattainable because they are beyond what is presently possible given the country's scarce resources. But such points are desirable because they mean more output and consumption of both goods.

Straight-line versus curved PPCs
A PPC can be either straight or bowed outwards from the origin

A straight line PPC
- Indicates that the two goods require similar resources to produce (like pizzas and calzones)
- The opportunity cost of one pizza is one calzone, so Italy always gives up the same quantity of one good no mater where it is on its PPC

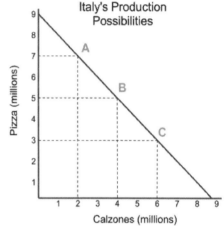

A bowed out PPC
- Indicates that the two goods require very different resources to produce (like pizzas and robots)
- As Italy increases its output of one good, the opportunity cost (in terms of the quantity of the other good that must be given up) increases.

The Law of Increasing Opportunity Cost: As the output of one good increases, the opportunity cost in terms of other goods tends to increase

Key Concepts shown by the PPC
In addition to opportunity costs and tradeoffs, the PPC can be used to illustrate several other key Economic concepts, including…
- *Scarcity:* Because of scarcity, society can only have a certain amount of output
- *Actual output:* A country's actual output is shown by where it is currently producing on or within its PPC
- *Potential output:* A point on the PPC shows the potential output of a nation at a particular time
- *Economic growth:* An increase in the quantity or the quality of a nation's resources will shift its PPC out, indicating the economy has grown
- *Economic development:* The composition of a nation's output will help determine whether the standards of living of its people are improving over time

Central Themes in Economics

Having introduced several of the topics you will study in this course we can now look at some of the major themes that will underlie all sections of the course. These include:

Key Theme #1: The role of product and resource markets in the modern economy

In the market system, there exists interdependence between all individuals.
- Households (that's us) depend on the goods and services produced by business firms, and the incomes they provide us, for our survival
- Business firms depend on households for the workers, the capital, and the land resources they need to produce the goods they hope to sell us and make profits on.

These exchanges all take place in one of two categories of market present in all market economies

Product Markets	Resource Markets
Where households buy the goods and services we desire from firms. Examples: • The market for private schools • The market for dental services • The market for airline travel • The market for football merchandise	Where business firms buy the productive resources they need to make their products: • The market for teachers • The market for dentists • The market for pilots • The market for football players

In Resource Markets:
- Households supply productive resources (land, labor, capital)
- Firms buy productive resources from households. In exchange for their productive resource, firms pay households:
  - ➤ *Wages:* payment for labor
  - ➤ *Rent:* payment for land
  - ➤ *Interest:* payment for capital
  - ➤ *Profit:* payment for entrepreneurship
- Firms seek to minimize their costs in the resource market
- Firms employ productive resources to make products, which they sell back to households in the product market

In Product Markets:
- Consumers buy *goods and services* from firms
- Households use their money incomes earned in the resource market to buy goods and services
- *Expenditures* by households become *revenues* for firms
- Firms seek to *maximize their profits*
- Households seek to *maximize their utility* (happiness)

The Circular Flow Model of the Market Economy

Market economies are characterized by a circular flow of money, resources, and products between households and firms in resource and product markets. Notice:

- Money earned by households in the resource market is spent on goods and services in the product market
- Money earned by firms in the product market is spent on resources from households in the resource market.

The incentives of Households: *Maximize Utility*

The incentive of Firms: *Maximize Profits!*

Resource Payments (Incomes for households)

In exchange for their land, labor, capital and entrepreneurship, households receive payments. The payments for the four productive resources (which are costs for firms) are…

For Land: Rent	Firms pay households **RENT**. Landowners have the option to use their land for their own use or to rent it to firms for their use. If the landowner uses his land for his own use, the opportunity cost of doing so is the rent she could have earned by providing it to a firm.
For Labor: Wages	Firms pay households **WAGES**. To employ workers, firms must pay workers money wages. If a worker is self-employed, the opportunity cost of self-employment is the wages he could have earned working for another firm.
For Capital: Interest	Firms pay households **INTEREST**. Most firms will take out loans to acquire capital equipment. The money they borrow comes mostly from households' savings. Households put their money in banks because they earn interest on it. Banks pay interest on loans, which becomes the payment to households. If a household chooses to spend its extra income rather than save it, the opportunity cost of doing so is the interest it could earn in a bank.
Entrepreneurship: Profits	Households earn **PROFIT** for their entrepreneurial skills. An entrepreneur who takes a risk by putting his creative skills to the test in the market expects to earn a normal profit for his efforts.

Key Theme #2: The Price Mechanism

Prices are how resources are allocated between competing interests in a market economy. Without tradition or command determining the allocation of resources, prices send the signals to producers and consumers regarding what should be produced, how it should be produced, and for whom.

Examples of how prices allocate resources: Imagine a city with two types of street food, hot dogs and kebabs. How would price assure that the right amount of these two foods is produced based on consumer demand?

At present,

- The price of a hot dog is $2
- The price of a kebab is $3

Due to a report on the negative effects of hot dogs on health, consumers now demand more kebabs. How will each of the two systems assure that the increased demand for kebabs is met?

Prices are signals from buyers to sellers!
As the demand for kebabs rises, they will become scarcer, causing the price to rise. Sellers will realize there are more profits in kebabs and hot dog vendors will switch to kebabs.
The price mechanism led to a reallocation of resources!

Key Theme #3: The distinction between Economic Growth and Economic Development

The emerging market economies of the world have achieved amazing economic growth for decades; but at what cost? Is increasing income and output the only thing the market system is good for? Does getting richer assure we will be happier, live longer and healthier lives, and live in a just society? Two of the key areas of study in economics are those of growth and development. Sometimes these concepts are thought of as the same, but they are not.

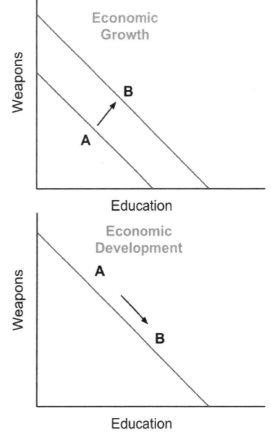

Economic Growth: This refers to the increase in the total output of goods and services by a nation over time.

- It is also sometimes defined as an increase in household income over time.
- It is purely a monetary measure of the increases in the material well-being of a nation.
- On a PPC growth can be shown as an outward shift of the curve.

Economic Development: This refers to the improvement in peoples' standard of living over time.
- Measured by improvements in health, education, equality, life expectancy and so on
- Incorporate income as well, but is a much broader measure than growth
- On a PPC development can be shown by a movement towards the production of goods that improve peoples' lives

Other Key Themes in the Economics Course: Throughout the course, the following themes will be considered across all areas of our study of Economics.
- *The role of government in the economy:* In every unit of this course we will examine the appropriate role of government in the market economy. There are some who argument government should never interfere with the free functioning of markets; on the other hand, when market failures arise, the government may be needed to improve the allocation of resources.
- *Threats to sustainability of current economic trends:* What threat do global warming, environmental degradation, population growth and urbanization play to the ability of our economic systems to endure?
- *The conflict between the pursuits of efficiency and equity:* Sometimes the pursuit of wealth and economic growth leaves some individuals behind. To what extent should economic policy be concerned with income and wealth inequality? Is there a mechanism available for reducing inequality while at the same time encouraging efficiency?

Chapter 2: GDP and its Determinants

The Circular Flow Model of income

- Explain why the total income and total expenditures in an economy are the same
- Distinguish between leakages and injections from and into the circular flow.

Measures of Economic Activity

- GDP as a measure of economic activity
- Three approaches to measuring GDP, output, expenditure and income
- Per capita GDP
- Calculating real GDP from data using a deflator

The Business Cycle

- Short-term and long-term fluctuations
- Long-run trend

Introduction to Macroeconomics

There are several key concepts from Microeconomics that are similar to some of the topics that will be covered in Macroeconomics. The table below shows several of the Micro concepts and their Macro equivalents.

Micro Concept	Macro Concept	Key Terms in Macroeconomics
Market	National Economy	Examines all the economic activity taking place in a country
Demand	Aggregate Demand (AD)	The total demand for a nation's output of goods and services
Supply	Aggregate Supply	The total supply of goods and services by all the industries of a country
Price	Average Price Level	An index of the average prices of goods and services over time
Quantity	National Output	Total output of all the industries of a country
Decrease in Demand	Recession	A fall in total output resulting from a decrease in AD
Increase in Demand	Inflation	An increase in the average price level resulting from an increase in AD
Decrease in Supply	Supply Shock	An increase in the price level and decrease in output from a fall in AS
Increase in Supply	Economic Growth	An increase in national output resulting from an increase in AS

The Macroeconomic Circular Flow
In the introduction to economics unit of the course, you learned about the circular flow of income in a market economy. In macroeconomics we have added several features to this model, including:

- A government sector: The government collects taxes from households and firms (these are a leakage from the circular flow) and contributes government expenditures on public goods (these are injections into the flow).
- A foreign sector: A nation spends money on foreign goods (imports, this is a leakage) and earns money by selling goods to foreigners (exports, an injection).
- The banking sector: Households and firms save money in the banking sector (a leakage) and banks provide households and firms with funds for investment (an injection)

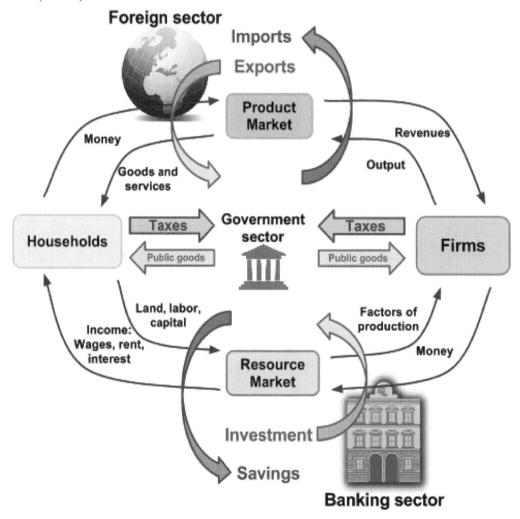

Leakage and Injections in the Circular Flow:
In the circular flow model above there are arrows indicating leakages from and injections to the circular flow.

- Leakages: Taxes paid to the government, spending on imports from abroad, and money saved in banks are all considered leakages from the circular flow of income. Any income earned but NOT spent on goods and services does not contribute to the nation's total output, and is therefore *leaked* from the nation's economy. However, these three leakages allow for the three following injections.

- Injections: Government spending, export revenues and investments are all enabled by the three leakages above.
  - ➢ Because households and firms pay taxes, government has money to provide the nation with valuable infrastructure, education, defense, support for health care and so on, all public or quasi-public goods that would be under-provided by the free market. These *contribute to national output* and are thus *injections* into the circular flow.
  - ➢ Because domestic households buy imports, foreigners have access to the money the need to buy the nation's exports. The spending by foreigners on domestically produced goods contributes to national output and is therefore an *injection*.
  - ➢ Because households save some percentage of their income, capital is available for others to borrow and spend. Spending on capital goods by firms or on homes by households (both considered investments) contributes to the nation's output and is thus an injection into the circular flow.

The total output of a nation's economy will either increase or decrease based on the relative size of leakages and injections!

Three Approaches to Measuring Output

Looking closely at the circular flow model, we can see that there is a relationship between the amount of income earned, the expenditures made and the total output. The economic activity of a nation can, in fact, be measures using any of these three methods:

The Income approach: Measures GDP by recording the income of household in the resource market side of the circular flow of income. Income includes payments households receive in the resource market in exchange for providing firms with the factors of production, including the total sum of each of the following earned by a nation's households in a year: *Wages for labor, Interest for capital, Rent for land and Profits for entrepreneurship.*

$$National\ Income = W+I+R+P$$

The Output approach: Measures the value of the total output produced in the different sectors of the economy. When the total output of every sector of the nation's economy is summed, total output is found.

$$National\ output = Outputs\ of\ the\ primary\ sector + the\ secondary\ sector + the\ tertiary\ sector$$

The Expenditure approach: Counts the total spending on final new goods and services in a given year. "Final" goods are ready for consumption and do not includes goods that will be input goods or are raw materials for other production. This approach distinguishes between four types of spending on a nation's output. These include *household consumption (C), investment in capital by firms (I), government spending (G) and net exports (Xn).*

$$Total\ expenditures\ equal = C+I+G+Xn$$

Introduction to Gross Domestic Product

The primary measure of the total economic activity of a nation is gross domestic product (GDP).

GDP = the total value of a nation's output in a particular period of time. Can be measured using the *income approach, the output approach or the expenditure approach.*

The measure of GDP we will use throughout our study of Macroeconomics is the *expenditure approach,* which measures the output of a nation by summing:

- C: The total spending by households on goods and services
- I: The investments firms make in new capital or that households make in real estate and homes
- G: The spending government does on public goods
- Xn: The spending of foreigners on goods produced by our country (exports) MINUS the spending domestic consumers do on goods produced abroad (imports)

The GDP of a particular nation in a particular year therefore equals the sum of C, I, G and Xn.

$$GDP = C + I + G + Xn$$

What is included in GDP?

GDP measures the *value of the final output of goods and services in a nation in a year.* But there are some economic transactions which are not included in GDP.

GDP includes:
- GDP includes only final products and services
- GDP is the value of what has been produced within the borders of a nation over one year, not what was actually sold.

GDP Excludes "nonproduction transactions":
- Purely financial transactions are excluded.
  - ➤ Public transfer payments, like social security or cash welfare benefits.
  - ➤ Private transfer payments, like student allowances or alimony payments.
  - ➤ The sale of stocks and bonds represent a transfer of existing assets (However, the brokers' fees are included for services rendered.)
- Secondhand sales: If I buy a used car in 2013, that sale does not count towards 2013 GDP, because *the car was not made in 2008!* The price of the car was originally included in the year's GDP when it was produced.

The Components of GDP
The expenditure approach to measuring GDP measures the total spending on a nation's output by households, firms, the government and foreigners. The four types of spending are outlined below:

Household Consumption (C): The purchase by households of all goods and services, including: • Non-durables: bread, milk, toothpaste, t-shirts, socks, toys, etc... • Durables: TVs, computers, cars, refrigerators, etc... • Services: dentist visits, haircuts, taxi rides, accountants, lawyers, etc…

Gross Private Domestic Investment- (Ig)
• All final purchases of machinery, equipment, and tools by businesses.
• All construction (including residential).
• Changes in business inventories
   ➤ If total output exceeds current sales, inventories build up.
   ➤ If businesses are able to sell more than they currently produce, this entry will be a negative number.

Government Purchases (of consumption goods and capital goods) - (G) • Includes spending by all levels of government (federal, state and local). • Includes all direct purchases of resources (labor in particular). • This entry excludes transfer payments since these outlays do not reflect current production.
Net Exports- (Xn): • All spending on goods produced in the U.S. must be included in GDP, whether the purchase is made here or abroad. • Often goods purchased and measured in the U.S. are produced elsewhere (Imports). • Therefore, net exports, (Xn) is the difference: (exports - imports) and can be either a positive or negative number depending on which is the larger amount.

Nominal GDP and Real GDP
Nominal GDP measures the value of a nation's output produced in a year, expressed in the value of the prices charged for that year.
* But if the average price level of a nation's output increases in a year, the *nominal GDP* could increase even if the actual *amount* of output does not change, since everything will *appear* more expensive at higher prices.
* To determine the change in the *real GDP,* (the actual output of a nation adjusted for changes in the price level), economists must measure the value of a nation's output in one year using the price level from a base year.
    ➤ In the case of the price level *increasing* (inflation): real GDP will be lower than the nominal GDP
    ➤ In the case of the price level *decreasing* (deflation): real GDP will be higher than the nominal GDP

Real GDP = the value of a nation's output in a particular year adjusted for changes in the price level from a base year. Offers a more accurate measure of actual quantity of goods and services a nation's produces because it adjusts for price changes.

Converting Nominal GDP to Real GDP
Study the output and price data for a hypothetical country in 2009 and 2010 below

Output in 2009	Quantity produced in 2009	Price in 2009	Total value of output 2009
Cheese	10	2	20
Chocolate	20	2	40
Watches	5	10	50
Nominal GDP in 2009:			110

Output in 2010	Quantity produced in 2010	Price in 2010	Total value of output 2010
Cheese	12	2.50	25
Chocolate	25	3	75
Watches	5	11	55
Nominal GDP in 2010:			160

To adjust a nation's nominal GDP in one year to its real GDP, we must measure the value of output using prices from a base year.

If we want to know the 2010 real GDP with 2009 as a base year, we must find the value of 2010's output in 2009 prices.
- *12 cheeses at $2 = $24*
- *25 chocolates at $2 = $50*
- *5 watches at $10 = $50*
- *2010 real GDP = $124*

The GDP Deflator= (Nominal GDP)/(Real GDP)
- For this country, the GDP deflator = 160/124=1.29
- With this we know that prices rose by 29% between 2009 and 2010.

Calculating real GDP using a GDP Deflator
The GDP deflator is a price index that can be used to adjust a nation's nominal GDP for changes in the price level. The deflator is an indicator of how much prices have changed between two years.
- For a base year, the deflator always equals 100, since the real GDP = nominal GDP
- If, in a later year, the index is 110, this means that prices have risen by 10% between those years. If it is 120, prices have risen by 20%. If it is 95, then price fell by 5%, and so on…

Consider the table below, showing nominal and real GDP data for the United States:

Year	Nominal GDP	GDP Deflator	Real GDP
2005	12,638.4	100	12,638.4
2006	13,398.9	103.25	12,976.2
2007	14,061.8	106.29	13,228.9
2008	14,369.1	108.61	13,228.8
2009	14,119.0	109.61	12,880.6

Notice that for each of the years from 2007 on, real GDP was lower than nominal because the deflator increased each year, indicating that there was inflation; therefore, nominal GDP would have over-stated the changes in real output from year to year.

Real GDP and Real GDP per capita
A nation's real GDP tells us the actual value of its output in a particular year, adjusted for any changes in the price level between that year and an earlier base year. However, real GDP does not tell us whether a nation is *rich or poor*. Consider the tables below:

Countries with largest GDP (and per-capita rank)	Total GDP, (trillions $)	Country with largest per capita GDP (and total GDP rank)	Per-capita GDP ($ in 2009)
1. United States (6)	14.2	1. Luxembourg (68)	105,350
2. Japan (14)	5.0	2. Norway (24)	79,089
3. China (86)	4.9	3. Denmark (29)	55,992
4. Germany (13)	3.3	4. Ireland (37)	51,049
5. France (12)	2.6	5. Netherlands (16)	47,917

Per capita GDP: Measures the total GDP of a nation divided by the total population.
- Gives a more realistic measure of how *rich* a nation is.
- Notice that none of the *richest nations* (on the right) are even in the top 10 for total GDP

Why is GDP important?

GDP is considered by economists to be the most important measure of economic activity in nations for several reasons:
- It tells us something about the relative size of different countries' economies
- It is a monetary measure, so it tells us *how much income* a country earns in a year (assuming everything that is produced is sold).
- When we divide GDP by the population, we get GDP per capita, which tells us *how many goods and services* the *average person* consumes in a country.
- When real GDP grows more than the population, that tells us that people *on average,* have more stuff than they did before.
- If you believe that *having more stuff* makes people better off, then GDP per capita tells us how well off people in society are.

Real GDP is a better indicator of output than nominal GDP

GDP per capita is a better indicator of the well-being of a typical person in a nation than total GDP

What are some shortcomings of GDP?

While GDP is a valuable and widely used measure of economic activity, it does have several shortcomings that must be acknowledged:
- It ignores all social aspects of human life, such as income distribution, access to health care and education, life expectancy, gender equality, religious freedom, human rights and so on.
- Certain important work is left out of accounting (homemakers, labor of carpenters who make own homes because GDP measures only the MARKET VALUE of output. GDP therefore is understated.
- GDP does not reflect that people in most countries work fewer hours than in past years (in 1900 the average work week in the industrialized world was 53 hours, today it is around 40)
- Does not reflect improved product quality
- Does not include the underground economy
- GDP does not put a market value/cost on the environment. Higher GDP may be accompanied by negative externalities, which are NOT subtracted from GDP.
- GDP does not tell us if the best combo of goods and services are produced; a machine gun and textbooks are assigned equal weight.
- Nor does it measure how GDP is distributed among the population
- GDP does not measure the total well being, happiness, a reduction of crime or better relationships with society, with other countries, etc…

Alternative Measures to GDP

While gross domestic product is the *primary* measure of a nation's output in a particular year, economists have developed alternative measures of output which are sometimes referred to instead of GDP. These include:

Gross National Product (GNP): Measures the total value of output produced in a year by the factors of production provided by a nation.

- Differs from GDP in that it includes output produced abroad by domestically owned factories, but subtracts output produced domestically by foreign owned factories.
- Does not offer as accurate a measure of the actual economic activity *within* a nation as GDP does, and is therefore not considered as useful as GDP for measuring output of a nation.

Green GDP: This is an under-used measure of economic activity which subtracts from real GDP the losses to the environment and biodiversity resulting from economic growth.

- Places a monetary value on environmental degradation and subtracts this from the nation's GDP
- It is a measure preferred by environmentalists who believe that economic growth overstates increases in peoples' well-being due to the fact that it ignores the externalities that accompany growth.

The Business Cycle

Changes in a nation's GDP over time can be illustrated in a simple economic model known as the *business cycle*. There are four stages to a nation's business cycle

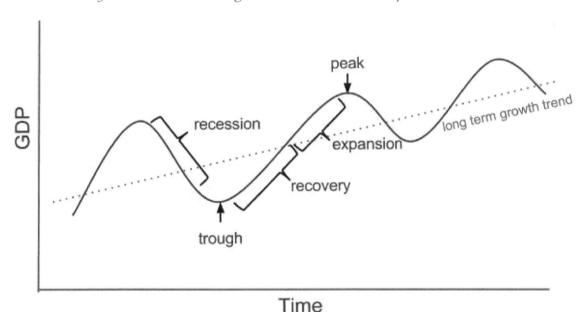

Phases of the business cycle:

- A recession is a decline in total output, income, employment, and trade lasting six months or more. During recessions, unemployment increases and there is downward pressure on the price level

- A recovery is when a recession has ended and national output begins to increase again
- An expansion occurs when an economy is growing at a rate beyond its long-run growth trend.

Long-run Growth Trend: Notice that despite the short-term fluctuations, the economy tends to grow over time

Notice from the business cycle model that economic growth (an increase in GDP) occurs over time, but not always at a steady rate. Of course, each economy's business cycle will look unique, but most economies will experience the types of fluctuations the model shows.

Possible causes of the business cycle
There are several theories regarding WHY countries grow at such volatile rates over time.
- Major innovations may trigger new investment and/or consumption spending.
- Changes in productivity may be a related cause.
- Most agree that the level of aggregate spending is important, especially changes in the purchase of capital goods and consumer durables.
- Cyclical fluctuations: Durable goods output is more unstable than non-durables and services because spending on latter usually cannot be postponed.

Decrease in GDP versus a decrease in GDP growth rate
- The growth rate of an economy refers to *the percentage change in GDP between two periods of time*. When an economy is approaching a peak in its business cycle, the *rate of growth* has begun to fall.
- When a recession begins, the actual output of an economy decreases. This means the growth *rate* has become *negative*.

The Macroeconomic Objectives
In our study of macroeconomics, we will focus on how the tools of macro can help policymakers achieve several objectives, all meant to make the lives of a nation's people better over time.

The four Objectives of Macroeconomic Policy:
1. Full employment: This means most of the nation's workers are able to find a job and that the nation's resources are being put towards the production of goods and services
2. Price-level stability: Inflation will be low, meaning households' real incomes are high. Unstable prices lead to uncertainty and unstable livelihoods for the nation's households
3. Economic growth: This is defined simply as an increase in output and income over time. Economic growth is needed to sustain a growing population and assure that the average person enjoys a higher standard of living over time.
4. Improved equality in the distribution of income: The free market tends to result in winners and losers. To some extent, the government must look after the losers in the market system, and implement policies that improve equality of income distribution so that there is less poverty in society.

Looking again at our business cycle model, we can see the effect of an economy which is successfully meeting its macroeconomic objectives.

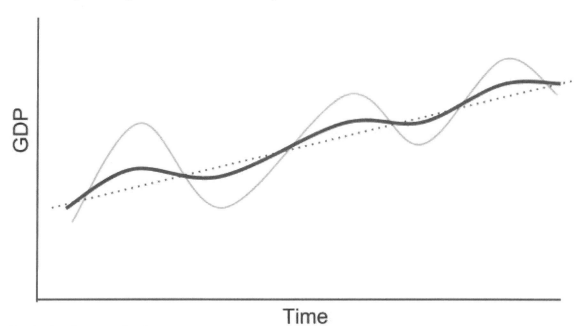

In the business cycle above:
- The bold line represents a more stable, steadily growing economy.
- Recessions are less severe, peaks and troughs less extreme
- Unemployment rises by less during recessions, and inflation is lower during expansions.

An economy meeting its macroeconomic objectives will achieve growth that is closer to the long-run trend line. There will be less volatility and uncertainty in the economy!

Chapter 3 – Aggregate Demand and Aggregate Supply

Aggregate Demand (AD)
- The AD Curve
- The components of AD
- The Determinants of AD and causes of shifts in the AD curve

The Keynesian Multiplier
- The meaning of the multiplier
- Calculating the effect of the multiplier
- Show the impact of the multiplier in an AD/AS model

Aggregate Supply (AS)
- The meaning of aggregate supply
- Alternative views of aggregate supply
- Shifting the AS curve over the long term

Equilibrium
- Short-run equilibrium
- Equilibrium in the new classical model
- Equilibrium in the Keynesian model

Introduction to Aggregate Demand

In microeconomics, the primary model used to show the interactions of buyers and sellers in market is the *supply and demand* model. In macroeconomics, we will deal with *total supply and total demand*. The model we will use to examine the interactions of ALL the buyers and ALL the sellers in a nation's economy is the *aggregate demand and aggregate supply model.*

Aggregate Demand: The total demand for the output of a nation at a range of price levels in a particular period of time from all consumers, domestic and foreign.

Similarities between Aggregate Demand and Demand:
- The curve illustrating both slopes downwards, showing an inverse relationship between how much is demanded and prices
- There are 'non-price determinants' of both demand and aggregate demand. Changes in these factor will cause the curves to shift
- A decrease in both causes employment and output to fall. A fall in demand will cause output and employment in a particular industry to decrease; a fall in aggregate demand will cause output and employment in an entire country to decrease.
- An increase in both causes prices to rise. A rise in demand will cause the price of a particular good to increase; a rise in aggregate demand causes the average price level in an entire nation to increase (inflation).

The Aggregate Demand Curve

The aggregate demand curve looks strikingly similar to a demand curve for a particular product. Let's examine the differences.

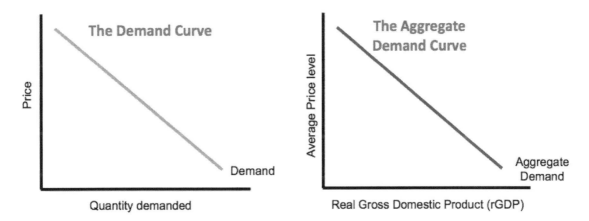

Notice the following:
- The AD curve shows the quantity demanded of the *total output (GDP) of the nation's economy while* demand shows just the quantity demanded for a particular good.
- The AD curve is plotted against the *average price level in a nation*, showing that at higher prices, less of a *nation's output* is demanded than at lower prices. Demand show simply the relationship between the price of a particular good and the quantity demanded of it.

Why does the AD Curve Slope Downwards?
The demand for a nation's output is inversely related to the average price level of the nation's good. There are three explanations for this:
- The wealth effect: Higher price levels reduce the purchasing power or the *real value* of the nation's households' wealth and savings. The public *feels* poorer at higher price levels, thus demand a lower quantity of the nation's output when price levels are high. At lower price levels, people *feel* wealthier and thus demand more of a nation's goods and services. (This is similar to the income effect which explains the downward sloping demand curve).
- The interest rate effect: In response to a rise in the price level, banks will raise the interest rates on loans to households and firms who wish to consume or invest. At higher interest rates the quantity demanded of products and capital for which households and firms must borrow decreases, as borrowers find higher interest rates less attractive. The opposite results from a fall in the price level and the decline in interest rates, which makes borrowing more attractive and thus increases the quantity of output demanded.
- The net export effect: As the price level in a particular country falls, ceteris paribus, goods and services produced in that country become more attractive to foreign consumers. Likewise, domestic consumers find imports less attractive as they now appear relatively more expensive, so the net expenditures on the nation's goods rise as price level falls. The opposite results from an increase in the price level, which makes domestic output less attractive to foreigners and foreign products more attractive to domestic consumers.

The Components of Aggregate Demand

A change in the average price level of a nation's output will cause a movement along the AD curve, but a change in other variables will cause the AD curve to shift in or out. The components of aggregate demand are the four types of *national expenditures*. These are:

- Household Consumption
- Capital Investment
- Government spending
- Net Exports

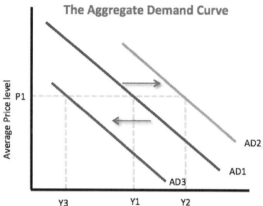

Assume a nation's economy begins at AD1:

- An increase in any of the four expenditures will cause AD to shift out to AD2, leading to a higher quantity of output demanded at P1.
- A decrease in any of the expenditures will cause AD to shift in to AD3, leading to a lower quantity of output demanded at P1.

Consumption (C)

As one of the components of aggregate demand, *consumption* refers to all the spending done by households on goods and services. The level of consumption in a nation depends on several factors.

The determinants of Consumption (C):	
Disposable Income	Refers to the after-tax incomes of households. As disposable income rises, C increases. If disposable income falls, C will fall.
Wealth	When value of existing wealth (real assets and financial assets) increases, households tend to spend more on goods and services. When wealth decreases, consumption decreases.
Expectations	If households expect prices or their incomes to rise in the future, then today C increase, shifting AD out. If they expect lower prices or incomes, then C will likely decrease, as households choose to save more for the hard times ahead.
Real Interest Rates	Lower real interest rates lead to more C, as savings becomes less appealing and borrowing to buy durable goods can be done more cheaply.
Household Debt	When consumers increase their debt level, they can consumer more in the short-run. But if household debt is too high, C will eventually decrease
Taxation	Higher taxes decrease disposable income and causes C to fall. A decrease in taxes increases consumption. Taxes are set by government as part of *fiscal policy*.

The Marginal Propensities

As national income rises or falls, the level of consumption among households varies based on the *marginal propensity to consume*. Besides consuming with their incomes, households also save, pay taxes and buy imports. The proportion of any change in income that goes towards each of these is known as the *marginal propensity*

- The Marginal Propensity to Consume (MPC): this is the proportion of any change in national income (Y) that goes towards consumption (C) by households: $MPC = \Delta C / \Delta Y$
- The Marginal Propensity to Save (MPS): The proportion of any change in national income (Y) that goes towards savings (S) by households: $MPS = \Delta S / \Delta Y$
- The Marginal Propensity to Import (MPM): The proportion of any change in national income (Y) that goes towards buying imports (M) by households: $MPM = \Delta M / \Delta Y$
- The Marginal Rate of Taxation (MRT): The proportion of any change in national income (Y) that goes towards paying taxes (T) by households: $MRT = \Delta T / \Delta Y$

Consumption is a component of AD, while savings, buying imports, and paying taxes are all *leakages* from the nation's circular flow. These three together are known as the *marginal rate of leakage (MRL)*. These are the four things households can do with any change in their income. Therefore,

$$MPC + MRL = 1$$

Calculating Marginal Propensities to Consume and Save

Study the table below, which shows how consumption, taxes, savings and imports change following a $1 trillion increase in US households' income.

Assume US household income increases from $10 trillion to $11 trillion				
Income:	Consumption	Taxes	Savings	Imports
$10 trillion	$7 trillion	$1.5 trillion	$1 trillion	$0.5 trillion
$11 trillion	$7.5 trillion	$1.6 trillion	$1.25 trillion	$0.55 trillion

- The Marginal Propensity to Consume (MPC)= $\Delta C / \Delta Y = 0.5/1 = 0.5$
- The Marginal Propensity to Save (MPS): = $\Delta S / \Delta Y = 0.25/1 = 0.25$
- The Marginal Propensity to Import (MPM) = $\Delta M / \Delta Y = 0.05/1 = 0.05$
- The Marginal Rate of Taxation (MRT) = $\Delta T / \Delta Y = 0.1/1 = 0.1$

$$0.5 + 0.25 + 0.05 + 0.1 = 1$$

Study the table below and then answer the questions that follow:

Line	Derivation of personal saving from the NIPAs:	1999	2000	2001	2002	2003	2004	2005	2006	2007
1	Personal income	7,802.4	8,429.7	8,724.1	8,881.9	9,163.6	9,727.2	10,301.1	10,983.4	11,667.3
2	Less: Personal current taxes	1,107.5	1,235.7	1,237.3	1,051.8	1,001.1	1,046.3	1,209.1	1,354.3	1,483.3
3	Equals: Disposable personal income (DPI)	6,695.0	7,194.0	7,486.8	7,830.1	8,162.5	8,680.9	9,092.0	9,629.1	10,184.0
4	Less: Personal outlays	6,536.4	7,025.6	7,354.5	7,645.3	7,987.7	8,499.2	9,047.4	9,590.3	10,131.7
5	Equals: Personal saving	158.6	168.5	132.3	184.7	174.9	181.7	44.6	38.8	52.3

Source: http://www.bea.gov/

1. Describe the changes in US personal income between each of the years from 1999-2007.
2. Calculate the *marginal rate of taxation* for each of the years (MRT=$\Delta T/\Delta Y$)
3. Calculate the *marginal propensity to save* for each of the years (MPS=$\Delta S/\Delta Y$)
4. Calculate the *marginal propensity to consume* for each of the years (in this table, consumption is referred to as 'personal outlays'. (MPC=$\Delta C/\Delta Y$)

Investment (I)

Investment is the second component of a nation's aggregate demand. Investment is defined as spending by firms on capital equipment or technology and by households on new homes.

The determinants of Investment (I):	
The Real Interest Rate	Interest is the cost of borrowing money. Firms will borrow more to invest in new capital when the interest rate is low, and invest less when interest rates are high.
Business Confidence	If firms are confident about the level of future demand for their products, they are more likely to invest now. If confidence is low, firms will withhold from making new investments
Technology	New technology tends to spur new business investment, as firms rush to keep their manufacturing techniques as modern and efficient as possible and to produce the latest goods and services that consumers are demanding.
Business taxes	When firms can keep a larger share of their revenues (i.e. when taxes are lower) they may invest more. Higher business taxes discourage new investments.
The degree of excess capacity	If a firm's factories have excess capacity (meaning they are currently producing below the level they are capable of) firms will be less likely to invest since output can be increased without acquiring new capital.
Expectations:	If firms expect prices of their goods to be higher in the future, they are more likely to invest now. If lower prices are expected, firms have less incentive to invest now.

The Investment Demand Curve *(for loanable funds)*
The real interest rate is the most important determinant of the level of investment in a nation. Study the graph below to understand the relationship between interest rates and investment.

The Investment Demand Curve: The graph shows the demand for *loanable funds*, which borrowers need to invest in capital or new homes. Notice:

- With a real interest rate of 8%, few firms will want to invest in new capital as there are very few investments with an expected rate of return greater than 8%
- When real interest rates are 3%, the quantity of funds demanded for investment is much higher, since there are more projects with an expected rate of return greater than 3%
- Firms will only invest if they expect the returns on the investment to be greater than the real interest rate (marginal benefit must be greater than the marginal cost)

Shifts in the Investment Demand Curve
As a component of aggregate demand, the level of investment in the economy depends primarily on the interest rate, but also on other determinants of investment.

If one of the determinants of investment changes, the level of investment will increase or decrease at every interest rate

- If business confidence improves, a new technology is developed, business taxes are lowered, firms are producing at full capacity or producers expect higher future prices, *Investment demand will shift from Di to D2*
- If business confidence worsens, business taxes increase, firms have lots of excess capacity or producers expect prices to be lower in the future, *Investment demand will shift from Di to D3.*

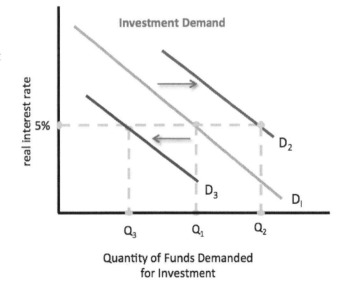

Net Exports (Xn or X-M)

Another component of the total demand for a nation's output is export revenues. Net exports refer to the revenue earned from the sale of exports to the rest of the world *minus* the expenditures made on imports from abroad. *Net exports equals exports (X) – imports (M)*

The Determinants of Net Exports (Xn):	
Foreign and Domestic Incomes	If the incomes of households in other nations rise, then demand for a country's exports should increase and net exports should rise. On the other hand, if domestic incomes rise, demand for imports will increase and net exports will fall.
The Exchange Rate	The exchange rate is the value of a country's currency relative to other currencies. As the exchange rate increases, a country's goods become more expensive and therefore less attractive to foreign consumers, while imports become cheaper, causing net exports to fall.
Protectionism	Protectionism refers to policies put in place by government intended to reduce amount of trade between one nation and others. Reducing protectionism will increase demand for imports in a country, and may cause net exports to fall. On the other hand, it may also increase demand for exports, causing net exports to increase.
Tastes and preferences	If a country's goods become more appealing to foreign consumers, demand for them will rise and net exports will increase.

Government Spending (G)

Government spending is the final component of aggregate demand. The level of government spending in a nation is determined by the government's *fiscal policy*.

Fiscal Policy: Changes in the levels of taxation and government spending meant to expand or contract the level of aggregate demand in a nation to promote macroeconomic objectives such as *full employment, price level stability and economic growth*. There are several key concepts relating to fiscal policy to consider:
- The government's budget: Changes in the level of government spending are reflected in the government's budget, towards which tax revenues go in order to finance government expenditures.
- Contractionary fiscal policy: If the government reduces its spending and / or increases the level of taxation, aggregate demand will decrease and shift to the left
- Expansionary fiscal policy: If the government increases its expenditures and / or decreases the level of taxation, aggregate demand will increase and shift to the right.
- Budget deficit: If, in a particular year, a government runs a *deficit*, meaning its expenditures exceed tax revenues, then government spending will contribute to AD that year and cause it to increase and shift out.

- Budget surplus: If, in a particular year, a government runs a *surplus*, meaning it spends less than it collected in taxes, then fiscal policy will subtract from aggregate demand, shifting it to the left.

Fiscal Policy's Effect on Aggregate Demand

In 2007 the US was about to enter a recession. In response, the government announced an *expansionary fiscal policy* aimed at increasing AD. The table below summarizes the components of and the desired effects of the government's policy.

Fiscal Policy Action	Desired Effect on AD
Tax rebates to 137 million people. A rebate of up to $600 would go to single filers making less than $75,000. Couples making less than $150,000 would receive rebates of up to $1,200. In addition, parents receive $300 rebates per child.	Lower taxes mean higher disposable income, which means more consumption, shifting AD out, increasing output and reducing unemployment
Business tax breaks. The bill would temporarily provide more generous expensing provisions for small businesses in 2008 and let large businesses deduct 50% more of their assets if purchased and put into use this year.	Lower business taxes increase the expected rates of return on investments, shifting investment demand out, increasing I, shifting AD and AS out (since there's more capital), increasing GDP and reducing unemployment
Housing provisions. The bill calls for the caps on the size of loans that may be purchased by Fannie Mae (FNM) and Freddie Mac (FRE, Fortune 500) to be temporarily raised from the current level of $417,000 to nearly $730,000 in the highest cost housing markets. It also calls for an increase in the size of loans that would be eligible to be insured by the Federal Housing Administration.	Since real estate is a major source of wealth for Americans, anything the gov't can do to increase demand for new homes will lead to an increase in home values, thus household wealth, a determinant of consumption. Higher home prices cause more consumption, stronger AD, more output and less unemployment

The Spending Multiplier and Aggregate Demand

When a particular component of AD changes (either C, I, Xn or G) the change in *total spending* the economy experiences will be *greater than* the initial change in expenditures. This is known as the *multiplier effect*.

Example of the multiplier effect in action: Assume the US government decides to increase spending on infrastructure project (roads, bridges, etc…) by $100 billion. What happens to this money?

- $100 billion will be earned by households employed in the infrastructure projects.
- Of that, some percentage will be *saved*, paid in *taxes* and *used to buy imports*. But some percentage will be *used for consumption*.

- Some of the income earned from the $100 billion of government spending is used to consume more goods, and therefore earned by other households as even more income.
- Assume that the MPC = 0.8. This means that of the $100 billion, an additional $80 billion of consumption will result as household incomes rise. There is now an additional $80 billion of new income, of which…
- $64 billion will be spent again (0.8 x 80). In this way, the initial change in government spending of $100 billion is MULTIPLIED throughout the economy to create even more total spending.
- *The size of the Multiplier is determined by the MPC, and can be calculated as:*

The spending multiplier (k)=1 / (1-MPC)

The table below shows the changes in total spending that will result from an initial change in expenditures of $100 in an economy, based on different marginal propensities to consume. Study the data and then answer the questions that follow.

Marginal Propensity to Consume	Initial change in Expenditures (C, I, G or Xn)	Size of the spending multiplier (1/1-MPC)	Total change in spending in the economy
0.2	+100	1.25	125
0.4	+100	1.67	167
0.6	+100	2.5	250
0.8	+100	5	500
0.9	+100	10	1000

Based on the data in the table above:
1. What is the relationship between the MPC and the size of the spending multiplier?
2. What is a logical explanation for this relationship?
3. Under what circumstance will a particular increase in government spending be most effective, when the MPC is low or when it is high?
4. Does the multiplier effect work when the initial change in spending is negative? What would this mean for an economy in which business confidence is falling?

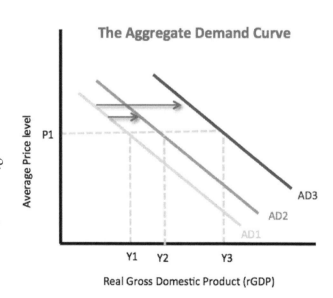

The Aggregate Demand Curve

Average Price level

P1

AD3
AD2
AD1

Y1   Y2   Y3

Real Gross Domestic Product (rGDP)

The effects of the spending multiplier can be seen on an aggregate demand curve. Assume, for example, an economy experiences $50 million increase in its net exports (perhaps due to a depreciation of its currency). The MPC in this economy is 0.6.

The Spending Multiplier = *1/(1-0.6)=1/(0.4)=2.5*

Initial change in spending = $50 million
  - The effect of the initial increase in Xn is shown by a shift from AD1 to AD2. At P1, the level of output demanded only increases to Y2

Final change in spending = $50 million x 2.5 = $125 million
  - The ultimate effect on AD will be a shift to AD3. Assuming the price level remained at P1, the total demand for output is now at Y3.

The Tax Multiplier and Aggregate Demand

When a component of AD changes, total spending will change depending on the spending multiplier. When a factor that *determines* one of the components of AD changes (taxes in this case), the effect on AD will be less direct.

The Tax Multiplier: When the government reduces taxes by a certain amount, households' disposable income increases, and therefore consumption increase, leading to an increase in AD. The tax multiplier tells us the amount by which total spending will increase following an initial decrease in taxes of a particular amount.

$$\textit{The Tax Multiplier (t)= (-MPC)/MRL}$$
$$\textit{or}$$
$$\textit{(-MPC)/MPS}$$

Remember, the MRL is the *marginal rate of leakage*. It refers to the things households do with any change in income that do *not contribute to the nation's total demand**.

Why two formulas? Two formulas are provided because in AP Economics, students are not expected to learn the MRL. The assumption is that MPC+MPS=1. However, in IB Economics, we must consider the MPS, MPM and the MRT, so MPC+MRL=1. The formulas are the same, but while IB students must divide the MPC by the MRL, AP students must only consider the MPS.

If we know the MPC for a country, and we know how much taxes are cut by, we can calculate the tax multiplier and determine the ultimate change in total spending that will result from the tax cut. *Remember that the MRL is always equal to 1-MPC.*

Marginal Propensity to Consume	Initial change in Taxes	Size of the tax multiplier (-MPC/MRL)	Total change in spending in the economy
0.2	-100	-0.25	25
0.4	-100	-0.67	67
0.6	-100	-1.5	150
0.8	-100	-4	400
0.9	-100	-9	900

Notice that at every level of MPC, the change in total spending that results from a $100 tax cut is LESS THAN the change in total spending that resulted from a $100 increase in spending (from an earlier slide). The tax multiplier will ALWAYS be smaller than the spending multiplier, since a proportion of any tax cut will be saved before it is spent.

Introduction to Aggregate Supply
As we have seen, the level of aggregate demand for a nation's output is determined by the four components of aggregate demand, which themselves are determined by many factors affecting domestic households and firms, foreigners, and the government's budget.
Aggregate Demand for a nation's output=C+I+G+Xn
- An increase in any of the four components will lead to a shift outwards of the AD curve
- A decrease in any of them will cause AD to shift inwards.

All that's left to determine the *equilibrium level of output* in a nation at a particular period of time is the *Aggregate Supply curve.*

Aggregate Supply: The total quantity of output of goods and services produced by the firms in a nation at a range of price levels in a particular period of time.

Similar to supply in microeconomics: Firms will respond to higher price levels by increasing their output *in the short-run* and to lower price levels by decreasing their output *in the short-run.*

The aggregate supply curve is generally upward sloping. However, there are competing theories that interpret its shape differently. For our analysis, we will consider the *short-run aggregate supply curve* and the *long-run aggregate supply curve.*

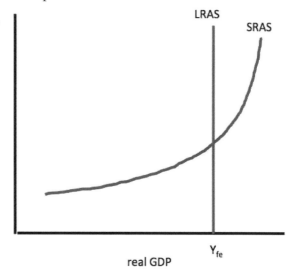

Short-run aggregate supply (SRAS): Illustrates the relationship between the price level of and the level of output produced in the *fixed-wage and price period*, which is the period of time following a change in aggregate demand over which workers' wages and prices are relatively *inflexible*.

Long-run aggregate supply (LRAS) illustrates the relationship between the price level and the level of output in the *flexible-wage and price period*, which is the period of time following a change in aggregate demand over which all wages and prices in the economy can adjust to the level of demand.

Background on the Competing Views of Aggregate Supply

The vertical, *long-run aggregate supply* curve reflects the theories of a school of economic thought known as the *new (or neo)-classical school of economics*. What follows is a brief background of the new-classical theory of aggregate supply.

The Classical view of Aggregate Supply: During the boom era of the Industrial Revolutions in Europe, Britain and the United States, governments played a relatively small role in nation's economies. Economic growth was fueled by private investment and consumption, which were left largely unregulated and unchecked by government.

When labor unions were weak and minimum wages and unemployment benefits were unheard of, wages fluctuated depending on market demand for labor. When spending in the economy was strong, wages were driven up and firms restricted their output in response to higher costs, keeping output near the full employment level.

When spending in the economy was weak, firms lowered workers' wages without fear of repercussions from unions or government requiring minimum wages. Flexible wages meant labor markets were responsive to changing macroeconomic conditions, and economies tended to correct themselves in times of excessively weak or strong aggregate demand.

The Classical view of aggregate supply held that left unregulated, a week or over-heating economy would "self-correct" and return to the full-employment level of output due to the flexibility of wages and prices. When demand was weak, wages and prices would adjust downwards, allowing firms to maintain their output. When demand was strong, wages and prices would adjust upwards, and output would be maintained at the full-employment level as firms cut back in response to higher costs.

In the new-classical view, the aggregate supply curve is always VERTICAL

The upwards sloping, *short-run aggregate supply* curve reflects the theories of a school of economic thought known as the *Keynesian school*. What follows is a brief background to the Keynesian view of AS.

The Keynesian View of Aggregate Supply: John Maynard Keynes was an English economist who represented the British at the Versailles treaty talks at the end of WWI. During the Great Depression, Keynes noticed that, in contrast to what the neo-classical economists thought should happen, the world's economies were not *self-correcting*.

Keynes believed that during a time of weak spending (AD), an economy would be unable to return to the full-employment level of output on its own due to the *downwardly inflexible* nature of wages and prices.

Since workers would be unwilling to accept lower nominal wages, and because of the role unions and the government played in protecting worker rights, the only thing firms could do when demand was weak was decrease output and lay off workers.

As a result, a fall in aggregate demand below the full-employment level results in high unemployment and a large fall in output. To avoid deep recession and rising unemployment after a fall in private spending (C, I, Xn), a government must fill the "recessionary gap" by increasing government spending. The economy will NOT "self-correct" due to "sticky wages and prices", meaning there should be an active role for government in maintaining full-employment output.

In the Keynesian view, AS is horizontal below full-employment and vertical beyond full employment!

The extreme Keynesian view of is seen as a *horizontal curve* and the extreme new-classical view of AS is seen as a *vertical curve*.

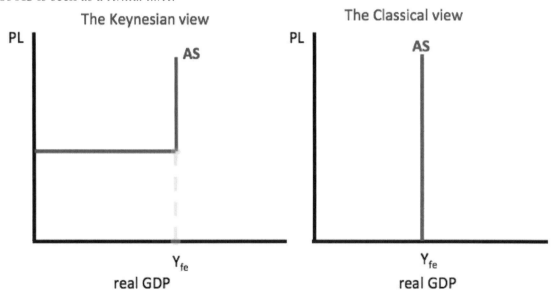

In reality, neither view is totally correct.

- Keynes was correct in the short-run, because wages and prices tend *not to adjust quickly* to changes in the level of demand.
- The new-classicals are correct in the long-run, because over time, following a decrease or an increase in AD, wages and prices tend to rise or fall accordingly, causing output in the nation to return to a relatively constant, *full-employment* level, regardless of the level of AD.

Short-run Aggregate Supply

The Keynesian theory of relatively inflexible wages and prices is reflected in the *short-run aggregate supply curve*, which is relatively flat below full employment (Yfe) and relatively steep beyond full employment.

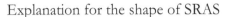

Explanation for the shape of SRAS

- Slopes upwards because at higher prices, firms respond by producing a greater quantity of output
- As price level falls, firms respond by reducing output
- At low levels of output (when unemployment is high), firms are able to attract new workers without paying higher wages, so prices rise gradually as output increases
- At high levels of output, when resources in the economy are fully employed, firms find it costly to increase output as they must pay higher wages and other costs. Increases in output are accompanied by greater and greater levels of inflation as an economy approaches and passes full employment

Long-run Aggregate Supply

The new-classical view of AS is reflected in the vertical, long-run AS curve, which shows that output will *always occur at the full employment level (Yfe)*.

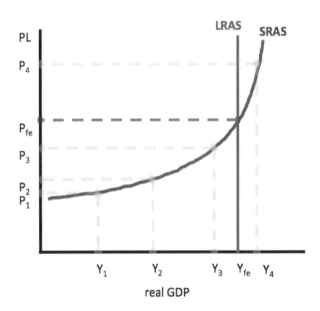

Explanation for the shape of LRAS

- AS is vertical at the full-employment level of output (Yfe), implying that whatever the level of AD, the economy will *always produce at full employment*.
- When AD is very low, wages and prices fall so that firms can continue to employ the same number of workers and produce the same output. *Output will not decrease when AD decreases*
- When AD is very high, firms will see wages rising and therefore they will NOT hire more workers, and will just pass their higher costs onto buyers as higher prices. *Output will not increase when AD increases*
- *Wages and prices must be completely flexible in the long-run for Yfe to always prevail*

The Determinants of Aggregate Supply

A change in AD is not the only factor that can lead to a change in an economy's short-run equilibrium level of output. AS can also shift, if one of the determinants of aggregate supply changes.

The Determinants of Aggregate Supply: When any of the following change, aggregate supply will either decrease and shift inwards (or up, graphically) or increase and shift outwards (or down, graphically).

- Wage rates: The cost of labor. Higher wages cause SRAS to decrease, lower wages cause SRAS to increase
- Resource costs: Rents for land, interest on capital; as these rise and fall, AS will shift in or out
- Energy and transportation costs: Higher oil or energy prices will cause SRAS to decrease. If costs fall, SRAS increases
- Government regulation: Regulations impose costs on firms that can cause SRAS to decrease
- Business taxes: Taxes are a monetary cost imposed on firms by the government, and higher taxes will cause SRAS to decrease
- Exchange rates: If a country's producers use lots of imported raw materials, then a weaker currency will cause these to become more expensive, reducing SRAS. A stronger currency can make raw materials cheaper and increase AS.

Short-run Equilibrium in the AD/AS Model – Full Employment

By considering both the aggregate supply AND the aggregate demand in a nation, we can analyze the levels of output, employment and prices in an economy at any particular period of time. Consider the economy shown here:

When equilibrium occurs at full-employment:

- The total demand for the nation's output is just high enough for the economy to produce at its full employment level in the short-run.
- Nearly everyone who wants a job has a job and the nation's capital and land are being fully utilized. Unemployment is at its *Natural Rate (the NRU)*
- Since the economy is at full-employment, we can assume that the macroeconomic objectives are being met:
    - ➢ Price level stability,
    - ➢ Full employment
    - ➢ Economic growth.

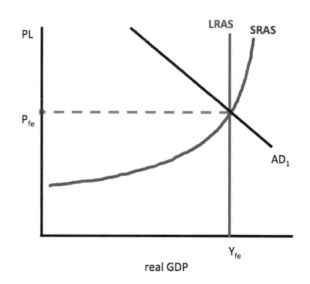

Short-run Equilibrium in the AD/AS Model – AD decreases

An economy producing at its full employment level is a *strong, healthy economy*. But what if something changed, and AD fell due to a fall in *consumption, net exports, investment or government spending?*

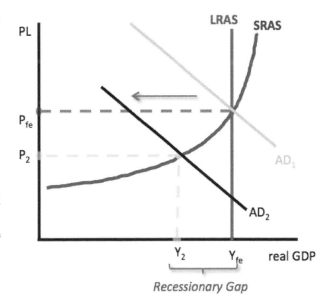

At AD2:
- A fall in expenditures has caused AD to decrease to AD2
- In the short-run, firms will fire workers and reduce output to Y2. Price level falls, but only slightly, to P2
- The economy is no longer at full employment, and is in a *demand-deficient recession* at Y2.
  - ➢ Price level has fallen slightly
  - ➢ Employment has decreased
  - ➢ National output has decreased, there is a *recessionary gap* equal to *the difference between actual output and full-employment output*

Long-run Equilibrium in the AD/AS Model: AD decreases

When AD decreases, output will decrease in the short-run because firms will have to lay workers off to cut costs and lower their prices. However, in the long-run, wages and prices are flexible, so output will return to its full employment level.

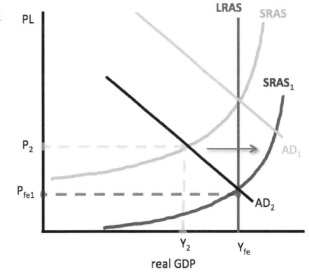

At AD2 in the long-run:
- Over time, unemployed workers will begin accepting lower wages, which will reduce production costs for firms
- At lower wage rates, SRAS increases to SRAS1, firms begin hiring back the workers they fired when AD first fell
- Output will return to Yfe, and prices will fall to P_{fe1}. The economy "self-corrects" in the long-run
  - ➢ Output returns to full employment
  - ➢ Wages are lower, but prices are too
  - ➢ The economy recovers on its own from the recession in the long-run

Short-run Equilibrium in the AD/AS Model – AD increases

Next let's examine what happens in the short-run when AD increases. Assume below that either *consumption, investment, net exports or government spending* increased, causing the AD curve to shift from AD1 to AD3

At AD3:

- An increase in demand led to firms wanting to produce more output, which increases to Y3.
- Wages are relatively inflexible in the short-run, so firms can hire more workers, and the economy produces beyond its full employment level.
- The economy experiences *demand-pull inflation*
  - ➢ Price level has risen due to greater demand for the nation's output
  - ➢ Employment has increased
  - ➢ The economy is beginning to 'overheat', and there is an *inflationary gap* equal to *the difference between actual output and full-employment output*

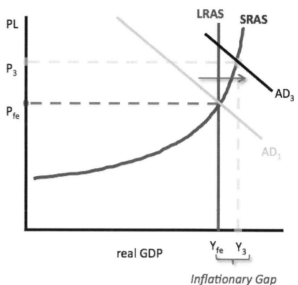

Long-run Equilibrium in the AD/AS Model – AD increases

In the long-run, wages and prices will adjust to the level of aggregate demand in the economy. When AD grows beyond the full employment level, this means wages will rise in the long-run, leading producers to reduce employment and output back to the full-employment level

At AD3 in the long-run:

- Demand for resources has driven up their costs (wages, rents, interest have all risen)
- Facing rising costs of production, firms begin reducing employment and output, and passing higher costs onto consumers as higher prices.
- Output returns to Yfe, and price level rises to P_{fe3}
  - ➢ The economy has self-corrected from the rising AD
  - ➢ Output is back at its full-employment level
  - ➢ There is more inflation in the economy (higher price levels)

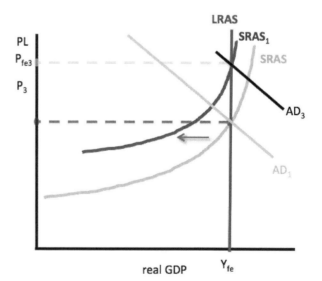

Negative Supply Shocks - Stagflation

Assume that a determinant of AS changes which causes the short-run aggregate supply curve to decrease, and shift to the left. What results is a situation known as *stagflation*

Stagflation: An increase in the average price level combined with a decrease in output, caused by a negative supply shock. "Stagnant growth" and "inflation" together make "stagflation"

- Assume higher energy costs caused SRAS to decrease to SRAS₂.
- To off-set higher energy costs, firms must lay off workers, reducing employment.
- Higher costs must be passed onto consumer as higher prices, causing inflation.
- An economy facing stagflation will only *self-correct* if resource costs fall in the long-run, which may occur if wages fall due to a large increase in unemployment.

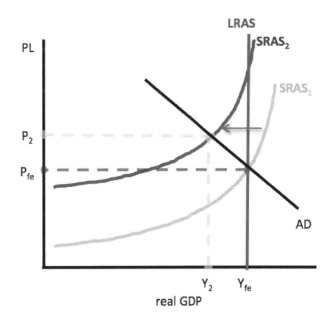

Positive Supply Shocks – Economic Growth

While a negative supply shock can be disastrous for an economy, a positive supply shock has very beneficial effects on employment, output and the price level. Assume, for example, a nation signs a free trade agreement and now lots of new resources can be imported at very low costs.

SRAS increases to SRAS₃:

- Cheaper resource costs allow firms to produce more output with the same amount of workers and capital.
- Lower costs are passed onto consumers as lower prices, Pfe falls to P3
- Output increases to Y3, indicating *short-run economic growth* has occurred.
- If the lower costs remain permanent, then eventually LRAS will increase and Y3 will become the new full-employment level of output, indicating *long-run economic growth*

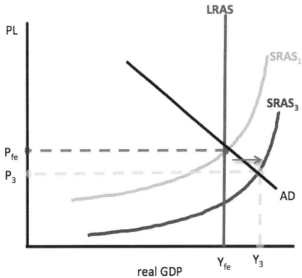

Long-run Economic Growth in the AD/AS Model
So far we have illustrated *demand-deficient recessions*, *demand-pull inflation*, *negative and positive supply shocks*. But real, long-run economic growth requires that not only AS or AD increase, rather that *both AS AND AD increase*.

Long-run Economic Growth:
- For national output to grow in the long-run, AD, SRAS and LRAS must all shift outward.
- This can be caused by an improvement in the production possibilities of the nation, combined with growing demand for the nation's output.
- The quality and/or quantity of resources must increase:
  - Better technology,
  - Larger population,
  - Better educated workforce,
  - More natural resources, and so on.

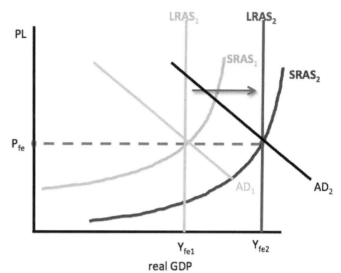

Chapter 4 – The Macroeconomic Objectives

Low Unemployment
- The meaning of unemployment
- Consequences of unemployment
- Types and causes of unemployment

Low and Stable Rate of Inflation
- The meaning of inflation, disinflation and deflation
- Consequences of inflation
- Consequences of deflation
- Types and causes of inflation
- Possible relationships between unemployment and inflation (The Phillips Curve)

Economic Growth
- The meaning of economic growth
- Causes of economic growth
- Consequences of economic growth

Equity in the distribution of Income
- The meaning of equity in the distribution of income
- Indicators of income equality/inequality
- Poverty
- The role of taxation in promoting equity
- Other measures to promote equity
- The relationship between equity and efficiency

Introduction to the Macroeconomic Objectives

The four objectives of macroeconomic policy are:
- Price level stability (low and stable inflation)
- Full employment (low unemployment)
- Economic growth, and
- Improved equity in the distribution of income

A nation's policy makers, both its government and its central bank, have several policy tools at their disposal to promote the achievement of these objectives. The different policy options will be explored in detail in a later chapter. In this chapter, we will go through each of the four macroeconomic objectives in detail, and determine:
- ➢ The meaning of each objective,
- ➢ The measurement of each objective
- ➢ The graphical illustration of each objective

The Meaning of Unemployment

Unemployment is defined simply as *the state of being out of work, actively seeking work, but unable to get work*. Note the following:
- Simply *not having a job* does not make an individual unemployed
- To be considered unemployed, an individual has to be of legal working age (this is between 16 and 65 in most countries)

- Being *under-employed* is different than being unemployed. Under-employment refers to individuals who are working part-time but wish to work full time, or to people who are working in a job for which they are over-qualified

Measuring Unemployment: To determine the extent to which unemployment is a problem for an economy, economists calculate *the unemployment rate*. This is the percentage of the total labor force that is unemployed

The Unemployment Rate (UR)=(Number of people unemployed)÷(Total Labor Force (TLF))×100

The Total Labor Force: This is the population of individuals in a nation who are of legal working age and are either employed or unemployed.

Calculating the Unemployment Rate
Consider the table below, which shows labor statistics for Brazil in 2010 and 2011.

Year	Total Population (millions)	Number of people Employed (million)	Number of people Unemployed (millions
2010	200	100	13
2011	208	102	15

From this data, we can calculate the following:
- The Labor Force Participation Rate (LFPR): This is the percentage of the total population that is part of the labor force (either employed or unemployed)
    In 2010 = 113/200×100–56.5%
    In 2011 = 117/208×100=56.25%
- The Unemployment Rate: The percentage of the labor force that is unemployed
    In 2010 = 13/113×100=11.5%
    In 2011 = 17/117×100=14.5%

The LFPR fell over this period, indicating that of the total population, a smaller percentage was working or trying to find work in 2011. May be an indication of a weak labor market

The UR increased over this period, indicating that it was harder to find a job in 2011 than in 2010. Even though more people are employed, there are even more unemployed

The data here indicates that Brazil's economy may have entered a recession in 2011. AD is not great enough to fully employ the available labor force in the country.

Types of Unemployment

Unemployment may take several forms, and arise from different macroeconomic conditions. The table below introduces the different types of unemployment and identifies their causes.

Types of Unemployment	Definition and Causes
Frictional Unemployment	Frictional or seasonal unemployment consists of those searching for jobs or waiting to take jobs soon; it is regarded as somewhat desirable, because it indicates that there is mobility in labor markets as people change or seek jobs.
Structural Unemployment	Unemployment arising due to changes in the structure of demand for labor; e.g., when certain skills become obsolete or geographic distribution of jobs changes; examples, Glass blowers were replaced by bottle-making machines. Oil-field workers were displaced when oil demand fell in 1980s, Airline mergers displaced many airline workers in 1980s, and foreign competition has led to downsizing in U.S. industry and loss of jobs.
Cyclical Unemployment	Unemployment caused by the recession phase of the business cycle; sometimes called demand deficient unemployment. Cyclical unemployment is caused by a fall in demand for the nation's output, which causes a loss of jobs in the economy.
The Natural Rate of Unemployment (NRU): An economy producing at its *full employment level* is expected to have only frictional and structural unemployment. If an economy has cyclical unemployment, it is in a recession and producing *below its full employment output level.*	

Causes of Unemployment

Unemployment can be caused generally by two factors: Either a *decrease in aggregate demand* or by a *decrease in aggregate supply*. However, the two natural types of unemployment have their own causes.

Causes of Cyclical Unemployment:

- Demand-deficient unemployment: If the total demand for a nation's output falls, firms will, in the short-run, reduce the number of workers they employ and reduce their output. This type of unemployment is known as *demand-deficient unemployment*, due to the fact that it arises from there not being enough demand for the nation's output.
- Unemployment caused by a negative supply shock: If the costs of production faced by a nation's producers suddenly rise, firms will employ fewer workers to try and remain profitable. National output falls and unemployment rises.

Causes of Structural Unemployment:
- If the technology used in production changes and becomes more capital intensive, the demand for workers who were previously needed to produce goods will decline
- If foreign countries can produce goods more cheaply, then domestic demand for certain types of labor will fall.
- If a nation's education and jobs training system does not prepare workers with the skills demanded in the labor market, structural unemployment will rise over time.

Causes of Frictional Unemployment:
- If unemployed workers cannot quickly and easily be matched up with firms that demand labor, then frictional unemployment will be higher and last longer than if it is easy for employers and potential employees to find one another

Illustrating Unemployment in the AD/AS Model
Using the basic AD/AS model, we can examine the level of unemployment in an economy relative and determine the types and causes of unemployment that exist.

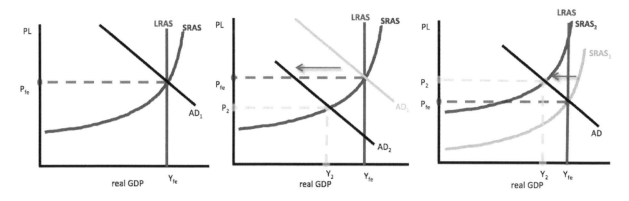

Natural Rate of Unemployment:	Demand-deficient Unemployment:	<u>Negative Supply Shock:</u>
• The economy above is producing at its full employment level	• The economy above is in a recession caused by a fall in AD	• The economy above has seen a spike in energy prices
• Unemployment is therefore at its natural rate	• There is cyclical unemployment	• Firms have reduced employment
• Only structural and frictional	• The UR is greater than the NRU	• The economy is in a recession and is experiencing high inflation too
	• There is a recessionary gap	

In addition to the three scenarios illustrated above, we can also show an economy experiencing an *unnaturally low level of unemployment.*

Here we see an economy in which AD has increased beyond the full employment level of output.

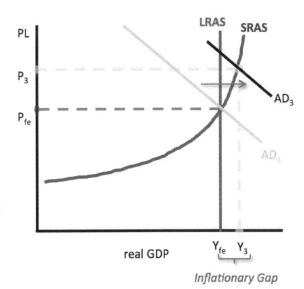

- The *inflationary gap* represents the difference between the equilibrium level of output (Y3) and the full employment level of output (Yfe).
- Firms in this economy are desperately hiring the few remaining workers there are available.
- At Yfe, there are only structurally and frictionally unemployed workers (the NRU).
- At Y3 unemployment is at a rate *lower than the* NRU. This is unsustainable.
- In the long-run, the shortage of workers will drive wages up and the economy will return to full-employment

Consequences of Unemployment

So why is *low unemployment* an important macroeconomic objective? This is because there are several harmful individual, social and economic consequences of an economy experiencing *high unemployment*. The table summarizes some of these consequences.

The Consequences of Unemployment	
For the Individual	• Decreased household income: reduces households' ability to buy the necessities and therefore reduces the standards of living of the unemployed • Increased levels of psychological and physical illness: Studies show that stress, depression, undernourishment, and other physical and mental effects arise from chronic unemployment
For Society	• Increased poverty and crime: There is a correlation between the level of unemployment in an economy and crime rates; the higher unemployment the more people will turn to crime to meet their basic needs • Transformation of traditional societies: Unemployment in rural areas of developing countries has risen as the global economy has changed the structures of these countries' economies, forcing traditional societies to adapt and in some cases dissolve as people seek work in modern industries.
For the Economy	• Lower level of AD: Households in which there are unemployed people earn less income and thus consume less, leading to less demand for goods and services in the economy. • Under-utilization of resources: A nation with high levels of unemployment is not achieving its production possibilities, thus peoples' standards of living are less than what is possible. • Downward pressure on wages for the employed: A large pool of unemployed workers increases the supply of available labor and thus reduces the wages offered to all workers.

The Meaning of Inflation

The second macroeconomic objective is *low and stable inflation.* Inflation is defined simply as *an increase in the average price level of goods and services in a nation over time.*

Measuring inflation: To determine whether a nation's price level is increasing or decreasing over a particular time period, economists use what is known as a *price index.*

- The Consumer Price Index (CPI): Measures the price of a set basket of consumer goods (usually includes hundreds or even thousands of goods that the typical household in a nation consume) between one time period and another.
- The Inflation Rate: Is simply the percentage change in the CPI between two years:

$$\textit{The inflation rate} = (CPI_{year\,2} - CPI_{year\,1}) / CPI_{year\,1} \times 100$$

Determining the CPI: The CPI for a particular year is the price of a basket of goods in that year divided by the price of the same basket in a base year.

To calculate inflation between two years, we first must determine the CPIs for the two years in question. Assume the CPI is made up of just three goods, whose prices during two years are indicated in the table below.

Good or service	Price in 2011	Price in 2012
Pizza	10€	10.50€
Haircuts	20€	19€
Wine	8€	10€
Total basket price	38€	39.50€

Determining the CPI: Assume 2011 is the base year, and we want to calculate inflation between 2011 and 2012
- CPI for 2011 = (Price of the basket of goods in 2011)/(Base year price)=38/38=1×100=100
- CPI for 2012 = (Price of the basket of goods in 2012)/(Base year price)=(39.5)/38=1.039×100=103.9

With the CPIs known, we can calculate the rate of inflation:

$$\textit{The inflation rate} = (CPY_{year\,2} - CPI_{year\,1})/\ CPI_{year\,1} \times 100 =$$
$$(103.9\text{-}100)/100 = 0.039 \times 100 = 3.9\%$$

Using a Weighted Price Index to Calculate Inflation
Because not all the goods measured in a nation's Consumer Price Index are equally important to the typical household, governments *weight* particular types of consumption more than other types.
- For example, food and beverages make up approximately 15% of the typical household's budget in a given year. But housing (either rental payments or mortgage payments) make up 40%.
- In this example, housing prices should be weighted more heavily than food and beverages

Consider the table showing the prices of the three goods measured in a CPI in two years, including the weight given to each good based on the percentage of the typical consumer's income spent on it.

Good	Price in 2009	Price in 2010	Weight
Banana	$2	$1.50	25%
Haircut	$11	$10	30%
Taxi ride	$8	$10	45%

To establish a price index with 2009 as the base year, we must calculate the weighted price of the basket of goods for 2009. To do this, we multiply the average price of each good by its weight, expressed in hundredths.

2009:

- Banana = 2 x 0.25 = 0.5, plus
- Haircut = 11 x 0.3 = 3.3, plus
- Taxi ride = 8 x 0.45 = 3.6
- *Price index for 2009 = 7.7*

2010:

- Banana = 1.5 x 0.25 = 0.375, plus
- Haircut = 10 x 0.3 = 3, plus
- Taxi ride = 12 x 0.45 = 5.4
- *Price index for 2010 = 8.775*

$$\text{Inflation rate} = (8.775-7.7)/(7.7) = 0.14 \times 100 = 14\%$$

Degrees of inflation

'Price level stability' is a primary macroeconomic objective; but what is considered 'stable' inflation? Is NO inflation (0%) desirable? What about negative inflation? We must distinguish between different degrees of inflation to know what is a desirable inflation rate.

Degrees of Inflation, from low to high	
Deflation:	Deflation refers to a decrease in the average price level of goods/services over time. • If the CPI for one year is smaller than the CPI from a previous year, then the inflation rate will be negative. • Deflation is considered highly undesirable because it discourages investment and consumption (households and firms prefer to postpone spending until prices are lower in the future) and therefore can lead to recession and rising unemployment.
Low inflation:	Inflation rates of between 0-5% are considered *low and stable*. • This is the desired range for most countries, over which consumers' confidence over the stability of future prices is sound; businesses and households can invest, spend and save without fear of future erosions in the values of their savings and investments.
High inflation:	Inflation rates of greater than 5% are considered high in most countries • At high inflation rates, firms and households will rush to spend their money now before its value is eroded by higher prices. The race to spend while money is dear causes AD to grow rapidly, causing *demand-pull inflation,* reducing real incomes and contributing to instability across the economy

Causes of Inflation

Inflation can be caused by one of two ways, either as a result of an *increase in aggregate demand* or as a result of a *decrease in aggregate supply*.

Demand-pull inflation: Occurs when there is an increase in total demand for a nation's output, either from domestic households, foreign consumers, the government or firms (C, Xn, G or I). When demand increases without a corresponding increase in aggregate supply, the nation's output cannot keep up with the demand, and prices are driven up as goods become scarcer.

Cost-push inflation: Occurs as the result of a *negative supply shock*, arising from a sudden, often unanticipated, increase in the costs of production for the nation's producers. Cost-push inflation could result from any of the following:
- Increase in the wage rate
- Increase in resource costs
- Increased energy or transportation costs
- Increased regulation by the government
- Increased business taxes

- Reduction in the exchange rate

Illustrating Inflation in the AD/AS Model

As with most macroeconomic concepts, inflation can be illustrated as an increase in the average price level in the AD/AS model.

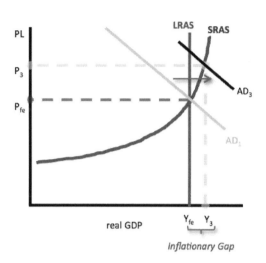

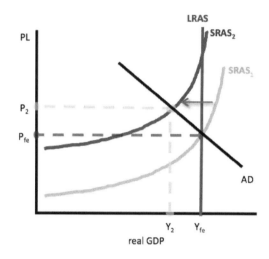

Demand-pull inflation:
When AD increases beyond the full-employment level of output the economy experiences an increase in the average price level

Cost-push inflation:
When AS decreases from the full-employment level, there is an increase in the average price level.

Consequences of Inflation

High inflation, like high unemployment, has several negative effects on households, firms and the overall economy.

The Consequences of High Inflation	
Lower Real Incomes	A households' *real income* is its nominal income adjusted for any inflation in the economy. The more prices rise, the less a certain amount of income can buy for households. Higher inflation makes consumers *feel poorer*, since the real value of their incomes falls when inflation rises.
Lower Real Interest Rates for Savers	The *real interest rate* is the *nominal interest rate* minus the inflation rate. For example, if you have a savings account offering a 5% interest rate, and inflation is 2%, the *real return on your savings* is only 3%. But if inflation increases to 4%, your real return is just 1%.
Higher nominal interest rates for borrowers	When banks anticipate high inflation in the future, they will raise the interest rates they charge borrowers today. This increases the cost of borrowing money to invest in new capital or to buy homes or expensive durable goods.
Lower real interest rates for borrowers	Inflation reduces the *real interest rate* for borrowers. The money paid back by borrowers is worth less than the money borrowed when there is inflation, thus the real interest paid is lower. Example: If a borrower faces a 5% interest rate on a loan, and the inflation rate increases from 2% to 3%, the real interest owed decreases from 3% to 2%.
Reduced debt burden for debtors	Similar to above, inflation erodes the real value of an individual's or a nation's debt. The value of the money owed by a debtor decreases as inflation increases.
Reduced international competitiveness	A country experiencing high inflation will find demand for its goods fall among international consumers, as they become more expensive compared to other countries' goods. Also, higher prices and wages will reduce foreign investment in the country as firms do not wish to produce where costs are rising, rather where costs will be low in the future.

Consequences of Deflation

Deflation, a decrease in the average price level, sounds like a good thing. But it is not, and in some circumstances can be worse for an economy than mild inflation. Here's why...

The Consequences of Deflation	
Rising Unemployment:	With the expectation of lower future prices for their output, and with low demand for goods and services, firms are likely to lay off workers, leading to higher unemployment and downward pressure on workers' wages across the economy
Delayed consumption:	With the expectation of future price decreases, households will increase savings and decrease spending. The decrease in current consumption can lead to further deflation and contribute to a *deflationary spiral*, in which lower prices lead to lower AD which leads to even lower prices
Declining investment:	If firms expect less demand for their output in the future, they'll invest less now, which could result in slower economic growth, as the nation's capital stock depreciates over time and is not being replenished at a rate that will promise sustained growth
Cost to borrowers:	Deflation causes the value of money to increase over time. Therefore, the real debt burden of borrowers increases as the price level falls. Bankruptcies result as borrower's incomes fall while the value of the money they must pay back increases.

The Relationship Between Unemployment and Inflation

As you may have noticed in our AD/AS diagrams, there is often a tradeoff between unemployment and inflation in an economy.

The unemployment/inflation tradeoff: When AD falls in the short-run, unemployment rises and inflation decreases (or becomes negative). When AD rises, unemployment falls and inflation increases. This *short-run tradeoff between unemployment and inflation is illustrated in a model known as the Phillips Curve.*

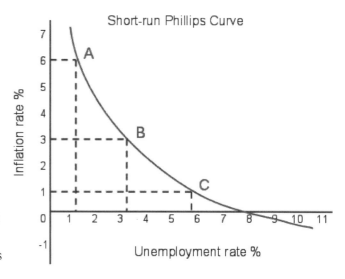

The Philips Curve: A graph that shows the relationship between unemployment and inflation in the short-run:

- At point A: Aggregate demand is

very high (probably beyond full employment) since inflation is higher than desired and unemployment is very low.

- At point B: AD has fallen to a level around full employment. Inflation is stable and unemployment is at a more natural rate of 4%
- At point C: AD has fallen, and the economy is probably in a recession. Inflation is very low and unemployment is relatively high.

The Short-run Phillips Curve and AD/AS

The Phillips Curve reflects the changes seen in an AD/AS model when AD changes in the short-run. Study the graphs below and observe how an economy *moves along its short-run Phillips Curve* when AD shifts from AD0 to AD3.

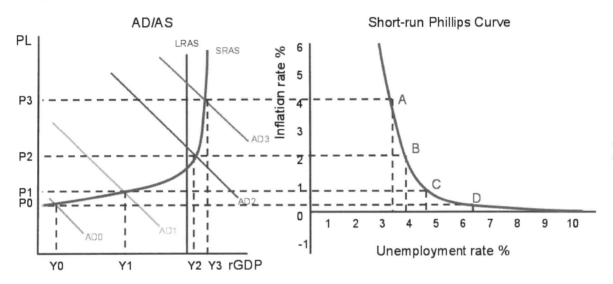

Rationale for the Phillips Curve Relationship

Why do inflation and unemployment move in opposite directions in the short-run? It all has to do with the amount of available labor in the economy at different levels of aggregate demand.

When AD is weak: If AD intersects SRAS at a level of output below full employment...

- Firms have cut back on output and reduced their prices to try to maintain sales during the period of weak demand. Inflation is therefore low.
- As firms have laid off workers, the number of people who are unemployed grows. Unemployment is therefore high.

When AD is strong: If AD intersects SRAS at a level of output beyond full employment...

- Firms have seen their sales grow and have begun raising their prices as a result. The nation's output is becoming more and more scarce, and consumers are willing to pay more, leading to inflation.
- In an effort to meet the growing demand for output, firms have begun hiring new workers, reducing the level of frictional and structural unemployment.

Supply Shocks in the Short-run Phillips Curve

As we have shown, a shift in AD causes a movement along the short-run Phillips Curve. However, a shift in SRAS will cause a shift in the short-run Phillips Curve. As seen below, a negative supply shock causes both unemployment and inflation to rise. This is seen as a rightward shift of the Phillips Curve.

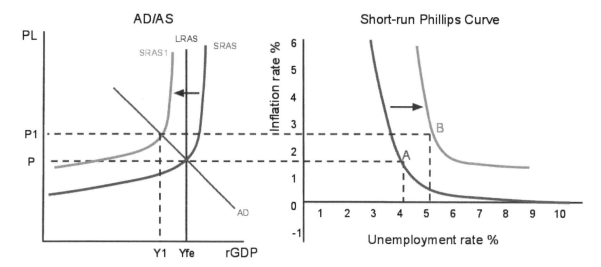

The Long-run Phillips Curve

In the long-run, you will recall, all wages and prices in an economy are flexible. Therefore, in the long-run, wages and prices of other resources and output will adjust to the level of aggregate demand, restoring a nation to its full employment level of output and unemployment at its "natural rate".

In the graph to the right, we can see...

- From point A to B: AD has increased, causing higher inflation and lower unemployment in the short-run. However, in the long-run, the economy will move...
- From point B to C: Because following the increase in AD, workers see their real wages fall and so eventually demand higher nominal wages. As they do so, firms reduce employment and raise prices, returning unemployment to its natural rate (NRU), now at a higher inflation rate.

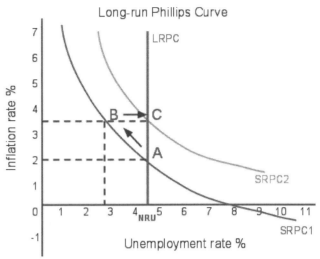

In the long-run, you will recall, all wages and prices in an economy are flexible. If there has been inflation in the economy, workers will demand higher wages in the long-run and employment and output will return to the full-employment level.

In the graph to the right, we can see...

- From point A to B: AD has decreased, causing lower inflation and higher unemployment. However, in the long run the economy will move...
- From point B to C: Because following the decrease in AD, workers who became unemployed eventually began accepting lower wages, leading firms to increase output and employment back to the full employment level

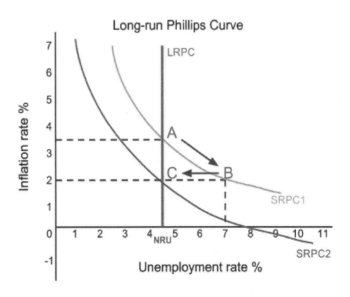

In the long-run, unemployment always returns to its Natural Rate, regardless of the level of inflation!

Introduction to Economic Growth

The third macroeconomic objective is *economic growth*, which is defined as an increase in the output of goods and services by a nation over time. Growth can also be defined as an increase in the *per capita income* of a nation over time.

- Growth in total output: Measures the change in the total output of a nation between two periods of time.
- Per capita economic growth: A better indicator of how the *average person* is doing, as it accounts for changes in nation's output AND the population.

Measuring Economic Growth: To determine the *economic growth rate*, we calculate the percentage change in a nation's GDP between two time periods:

$$Economic\ Growth\ Rate = (GDP_{year\,2} - GDP_{year\,1})/\ GDP_{year\,1}$$

Growth in actual output versus growth in potential output:
- If an economy is producing at a level of output below its full-employment level and output increases, then the economy's *actual output* is increasing. This is a type of economic growth that occurs during the *recovery phase* of the business cycle
- If an economy is producing at its full-employment level of output and output increase, this is the result of an increase in the nation's *potential output*, and is a form of *long-run economic growth*.

With the formula above, we can easily calculate the growth rate of an economy between two periods of time. Consider the data for Switzerland's GDP in the table below.

Year	2008	2009	2010
GDP (billions of $)	474	465	499
GDP Growth Rate	-	(465-474)/474= -0.019×100=**-1.9**%	(499-465)/465= 0.073×100=**7.3**%

Notice from the calculations:
- Between 2008 and 2009, Switzerland's GDP declined, giving the country a *negative growth rate*. If Economic growth is negative, the country is in a recession, as was Switzerland in 2009.
- Between 2009 and 2010, Switzerland's growth rate is much higher, at 7.3%. During this year, Switzerland was in the *recovery phase* of its business cycle, since it was just coming out of a recession.
- Since the 7.3% increase in 2010 is greater than the 1.9% decrease in 2009, we can assume that both Switzerland's *actual output* and its *potential output* grew in 2010.

Illustrating Economic Growth – three Models
Economic growth can be illustrated using three models we have learned already: the PPC, the business cycle and the AD/AS model.

The AD/AS model: Short-run growth is shown as an outward shift in AD, long-run growth by an outward shift in AD and AS.

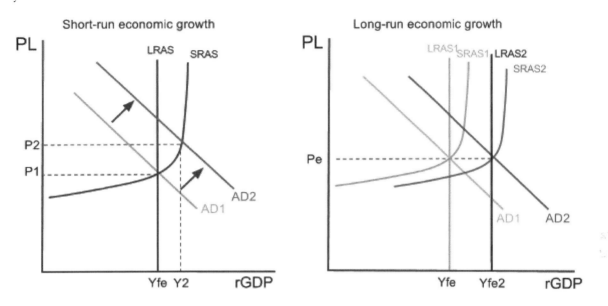

The Business Cycle: Short-run growth is shown as periods of recovery and expansion, long-run growth as an increase in output over time

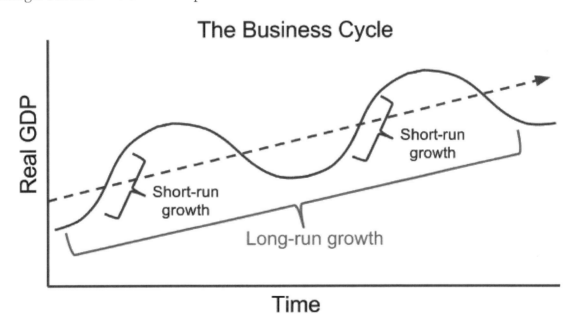

The PPC: Short-run growth is shown as a movement from point X to points A or B, long-run grown as a movement of the PPC outwards (from points A or B to point C)

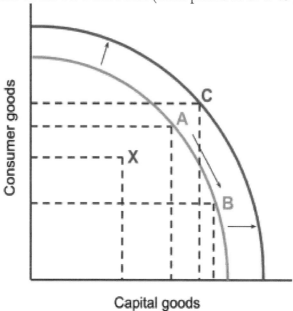

Sources of Economic Growth

Growth increases household income and contributes to the standard of living of the average citizen in a country. For these reasons, it is considered an important macroeconomic objective. But what are the sources of economic growth?

Sources of Long-run Economic Growth	
Physical Capital and Technology	A nation's stock of physical capital is the quantity and quality of technology and infrastructure in a nation • Physical capital includes computer and communication technologies, high speed Internet access, efficient transportation networks, sanitation infrastructure and so on. • Physical capital is only accumulated through INVESTMENT, either by the private sector or by the government. The private sector tends to provide ample investment in technologies that can easily be marketed and sold for a profit, while the public sector is needed to provide the public and merit goods that are necessary to make an economy grow: those things that would be under-provided by the free market, such as roads, ports, rail lines, communications infrastructure and so on.
Human Capital and Productivity	Human capital refers to the quality of the labor force in a nation. Human capital can be improved through education and training of the nation's workforce, which may be undertaken by either the private sector or the government, or as is often the case, by both. • The quality of the education provided by a nation's school system determines the quality of the human capital produced, and therefore the productivity of workers. • Greater skills among workers, and access to technology, increase the output per worker, and therefore the average income of households in a nation.

Consequences of Economic Growth

The most obvious effect of economic growth is HIGHER INCOMES and GREATER OUTPUT, both which benefit the households and firms in a nation. However, there are several *undesirable* consequences that may arise from the growth in output of a nation over time. These include:

- Externalities: Economic growth often comes at the expense of the environment. If growth is fueled by resource depletion, it may be unsustainable and may result in harmful effects on human and environmental health.
- Inflation: In economies experiencing rapid growth, high inflation often accompanies it. This means that if household incomes do not keep up with inflation, higher incomes may not actually improve standards of living over time. To adjust for inflation, it is important to consider the *real economic growth per capita* to determine how much better or worse off the typical household is from growth.
- Structural unemployment: A common effect of growth in the era of globalization is large numbers of people becoming *structurally unemployed*, as certain skills are no

longer demanded in rapidly growing economies. An example is the disappearance of manufacturing jobs in the West as Asian nations attracted most new investment by manufacturers due to lower labor costs.

- Composition of output: If growth is primarily because of higher output in sectors that detract from human welfare (such as the weapons industry), then it may not make the typical household better off.
- Unequal distribution of income: the benefits of growth may not be shared across all segments of society, particularly if the rich see incomes rise dramatically while the middle class stagnates.

Introduction to Equity of Income Distribution

The final macroeconomic objective we will discuss is that of *equity in the distribution of income*. As mentioned already, one of the possible consequences of economic growth in a free market economy is inequality in the distribution of income.

Equity versus Equality: There is a difference between these two terms.

- Equality in income distribution would mean that everyone earns the same amount, regardless of what skills he or she provides to the labor market. This was an objective of *socialist economies* based on the *communist system* of economics. This, however, is not an objective of a modern, market economy.
- Equity refers to *fairness* in the distribution of income.
  - ➢ Increased *fairness* can be achieved through macroeconomic policies that, for example, place higher tax rates on higher income earners than on lower income earners, and
  - ➢ Through fiscal policies that redistribute the nation's income through *transfer payments* and spending on *public goods* in a way that provides *equal opportunity* for all members of society to earn a decent income, the government can promote greater equity.

Measuring Income Equality: To measure the income equality of a nation, economists use a model known as the *Lorenz Curve*, which shows the percentage of total income earned by the different segments of a nation's population

The Lorenz Curve model plots the percentage of a nation's total income against the percentage of the nation's population, and thereby shows how much each *quintile* (or one fifth) of the population earns of the total income. Consider the table below:

% Of Population	Poorest 20%	2nd 20%	3rd 20%	4th 20%	Richest 20%	Gini Index
Cambodia	6.5%	9.7%	12.9%	18.9%	52%	43
Indonesia	7.4%	11%	14.9%	21.3%	45.5%	39.4
Brazil	3%	6.9%	11.8%	19.6%	58.7%	56.7
Vietnam	7.1%	10.8%	15.2%	21.6%	45.4%	37
Turkey	5.4%	10.3%	15.2%	22%	47.1%	41

The table shows us the percentages of total income earned by each quintile of the populations of several countries. From this data we can observe:

- Brazil is the *least equal country* on the list, because the poorest people earn a smaller proportion of total income relative to the richest compared to any other country.
- Indonesia and Vietnam are the *most equal countries* on the list. The poorest 20% earn a larger proportion relative to the richest 20% compared to the other countries.

The data from the table can be plotted in a Lorenz Curve Diagram

Illustrating Income Distribution in a Lorenz Curve Model
Let's take one country from the table, Cambodia, and plot the data on a graph with the *percentage of the population* on the horizontal axis and *cumulative percentage of total income* on the vertical axis. This is our Lorenz Curve model

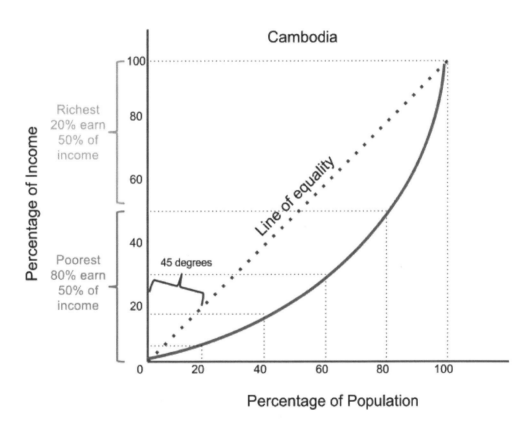

The curved line is Cambodia's Lorenz Curve:
- It shows that the poorest 20% earn just 6.5% of total income, while the riches 20% earn over 50% of income.
- The 'line of equality' is for comparison; a country with a Lorenz Curve along this line would be totally equal, with everyone earning the same amount.
- The further a country's Lorenz Curve is from the line of equality, the more *unequally* income is distributed.
- The closer the Lorenz Curve to the line of equality *the more equally* income is distributed.

The Gini Coefficient as an Indicator of Income Inequality
Because it would be inefficient to always draw a Lorenz Curve when comparing the levels of income equality across countries, economists have devised a numerical indicator of equality, known as the Gini Coefficient.

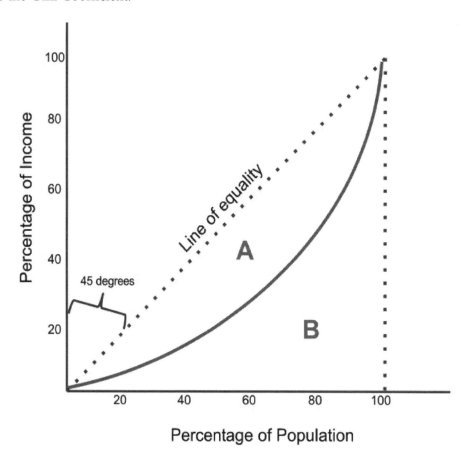

Percentage of Population

The Gini Coefficient: The ratio of the area below the line of equality and the Lorenz Curve and the entire area below the line of quality.
- Notice that the further away the Lorenz Curve is from the line of equality, the greater A will be relative to B, and therefore the higher the Gini Coefficient will be.
- The closer the curve to the line of equality, the smaller A will be relative to B, and the lower the Gini Coefficient will be.
- The closer the coefficient is to ZERO, the *more equal* a country is. The closer it is to ONE, the *less equal* the country is

Comparing Income Distributions using Lorenz Curves
By comparing the Lorenz Curves and Gini Coefficients of different countries, we can draw conclusions about the levels of income inequality.

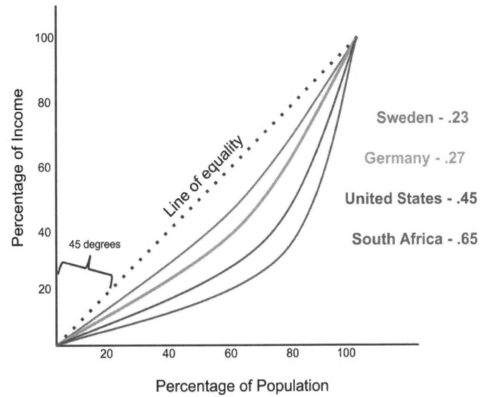

Percentage of Population

From the Diagram, we can conclude:

- Sweden is the country in which income is distributed *most evenly*.
- South Africa is the country in which income is distributed *least evenly*.

Sources of Income Inequality: Why would one country be more equal than another?

- The primary answer lies in the extent to which the government of Sweden promotes equity in income distribution compared to the government of South Africa.
- Income inequality is a market failure, which without government intervention will be rampant in a free market economy.

Relative versus Absolute Poverty

Without certain government policies to promote equity, a free market economy will ultimately create a society in which there is a vast gap between the richest and the poorest households. This will likely result in *poverty:* both *relative poverty* and, in the poorest countries, *absolute poverty*.

Relative poverty: When certain households in a nation earn an income that makes them poor relative to the richer households in a nation. Relative poverty exists in even the richest countries, and while individuals may be able to afford the basic necessities of life, their standards of living will be significantly lower than the relatively rich within their societies.

Absolute poverty: When a household earns an income that is below a level that allows them to buy even the basic necessities of life (nutritious food, shelter, clothing, education and health).

- The World Bank defines the absolute poverty line as $2 per day. There are approximately 1 billion individuals in the world living in absolute poverty in 2012, mostly in Sub-Saharan Africa, parts of Central Asia and parts of Latin America.
- Unlike relative poverty, which exists everywhere, there is little or no absolute poverty in the more developed countries in the world.

The Role of Government in Promoting Equity - Taxes
Certain government interventions in the free market can promote equity, or fairness, in a market economy, and thus, indirectly, reduce the level of income inequality in a nation. Policies include the taxes a government collects and the transfer payments and public goods it provides.

A tax can be either regressive, proportional or progressive:	
Regressive taxes	A tax that consist of a larger percentage of poor household's income than a rich household's income. • Indirect taxes are regressive: A tax on consumption of a particular percentage places a larger burden on a poor consumer than on a rich consumer. For example, a 10% tax on a $100 good is $10. To a poor household, $10 is a much bigger deal than to a rich household. • A government that uses indirect taxes as its primary revenue source will actually *worsen income inequality in society* since they place a smaller burden on the rich than on the poor.
Proportional taxes	This is a tax that remains constant as a proportion of income as incomes increase. A direct tax (on income) may be a *flat tax*, for example, all households pay 15% of their income in tax, regardless of the income level. Proportional taxes do *nothing* to promote income equality, although they will not *worsen inequality*
Progressive taxes	A tax that *increases as a percentage of total income as income increases*. For example, households earning $50,000 may pay only 10% in income tax, while those earning $250,000 may pay 35% in taxes. A progressive tax promotes *greater income equality* because those who can *afford to pay the most* do, and those whose incomes are lower and cannot afford to pay as much *pay less,* leaving poorer households with more disposable income to enable a higher standard of living.

The Role of Taxes

A progressive income tax is the most proven method for reducing income inequality.

It is not a coincidence that the *most equal countries in the world (Sweden, Denmark, Norway, France, the Netherlands)* have some of the *most progressive tax systems.*

Study the graph, which shows the amount of tax paid relative to income under the three systems:

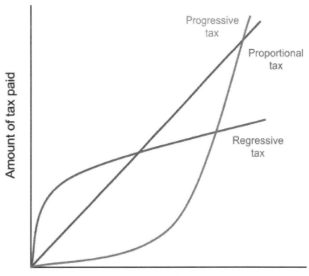

- Regressive taxes: Rich pay MORE total tax (since they consume more than the poor), but as a proportion of their income they pay LESS as their incomes rise (since richer households tend to save a larger proportion of their incomes than poor households)
- Proportional taxes: Sometimes called 'fair taxes' because everyone pays the same percentage. But under such a system the tax system does not increase equality or provide greater equity through the government
- Progressive taxes: Increase exponentially as income increases. Arguments against this say it discourages hard work, because the more income you earn, the more you have to pay in tax. But this system does the most to promote equity and equality in income distribution

The Role of Transfer Payments

The method a government uses to collect taxes (direct or indirect, regressive or progressive) only provides us with half the explanation of how government can promote equity. The other half of the equation is how the government *spends its money.*

Transfer payments: A transfer payment is a payment from the government to an individual for which no good or service is exchanged, rather income is redistributed from one group to another.

- The government's provision of transfer payments is intended primarily to provide greater equity through increased opportunities for low income households.
- Examples of equity-enhancing transfer payments include:
  ➢ Unemployment benefits: To limit the fall in income experienced by individuals who lose their jobs
  ➢ Social Security: To provide income to individuals in old age; reduces poverty among elderly
  ➢ Nutritional subsidies: To help low income households afford healthier food and improve health

➢ Educational subsidies: To help low income households afford a college education
➢ Health care subsidies: To reduce the cost of health care for lower income individuals
➢ Welfare benefits: To provide the poorest of households with an income so they can purchase the basic necessities

Chapter 5 – Fiscal Policy
The Government Budget
- Sources of government revenue
- Types of government expenditures
- The budget outcome

The Role of Fiscal Policy
- Fiscal policy and short-term demand management
- The impact of automatic stabilizers
- Fiscal policy and its impact on potential output
- Evaluation of Fiscal Policy

Introduction to Fiscal Policy
In an effort to promote the macroeconomic objective (price level stability, economic growth and full employment) policy-makers have a variety of tools at their disposal. One set of tools is known as *fiscal policy*.

Fiscal Policy: Changes in the level of government spending and taxation aimed at either increasing or decreasing the level of aggregate demand in an economy to promote the macroeconomic objectives. Fiscal policy is a type of *demand-side policy*

- The economy in the upper graph is producing at full-employment. Therefore, there is no in need for any fiscal policy actions, however…
- The economy in the bottom graph is in a recession and could therefore benefit from *expansionary demand-side policies* that increase AD and therefore employment and output closer to the full employment level.
- If AD is too high and there is high inflation an economy could benefit from *contractionary demand-side policies* that reduce AD.

The Government Budget – Sources of Revenue
Fiscal policy puts the government's budget into action to stimulate or contract AD as needed. The budget is simply the combination of revenues earned from taxes and expenditures made by all goods and services by nation's government in a year.

Tax revenues: A government's primary source of revenues is through the collection of taxes.

- Direct taxes: Taxes on incomes earned by households and firms. These are usually progressive in nature, meaning that the percentage paid increases as income increases, or proportional, meaning that all individuals (or firms) pay the same percentage no matter what their income.
- Indirect taxes: Taxes on consumption are *indirect*, meaning they are actually paid by the sellers of goods, but they are born by both producers and consumers.

Other sources of revenue: To a lesser extent, a government may earn revenue from:
- The sale of goods and services,
- The sale of government property,
- The privatization of state-owned enterprises to private sector investors

The Government Budget – Types of Expenditures

While a government's revenues come from the taxes it collects. Its expenditures depend on the goods and services the government provides the nation. Government expenditures include:
- Current Expenditures: This is the day to day cost of running the government. The wages and salaries of public employees, including in local, state and national government, such as police, teachers, legislatures, military servicemen, judges, etc…
- Capital Expenditures: These are investments made by the government in capital equipment and infrastructure, such as money spent on roads, bridges, schools, hospitals, military equipment, courthouses, etc...
- Transfer payments: This type of government spending does not contribute to GDP (unlike those above), because income is only *transferred* from one group of people to another in the nation. Includes welfare and unemployment benefits, subsidies to producers and consumers, etc… Money transferred by the government from one group to another, without going towards the provision of an actual good or service.

The Government Budget – Surpluses and Deficits

In a particular year, a government's budget can either be *balanced, in surplus or in deficit*. The net effect on aggregate demand depends on the government's budget balance.
- A balanced budget: A government's budget is in balance if its expenditures in a year equal its tax revenues for that year. A balanced budget will have no net effect on aggregate demand since the *leakages (taxes collected) equal the injections (expenditures made)*.
- A budget surplus: If, in a year, the government collects MORE in taxes than it spends, the budget is in *surplus*. A surplus may sound like a good thing, but in fact the net effect of a budget surplus on AD is negative, since *leakages exceed injections*. *A budget surplus will reduce the national debt.*
- A budget deficit: If a government's expenditures in a year are greater than the tax revenue it collects, the government's budget is in *deficit*. A deficit has a positive net effect on AD, since *injections exceed leakages* from the government sector. *A budget deficit will add to the national debt.*
- The national debt: A nation's debt is the sum of all its past deficits minus its past surpluses. If this number is negative, then it means the government has borrowed money over the years to finance its deficits that it has not paid back through accumulated surpluses

The Role of Fiscal Policy – During a Recession

If an economy has experienced a fall in aggregate demand, it might be in a *demand-deficient recession*. To combat such a slump in economic activity, a government can use *expansionary fiscal policies*

Assume an economy is experiencing a recessionary gap as seen here:

- Private spending in the economy has fallen (C, I or Xn)
- To make up the gap, the government can attempt to use *expansionary fiscal policies*. These include:
  - ➤ A reduction in taxes, and / or
  - ➤ An increase in government spending
- The size of the tax cut or increase in government spending needed depends on two factors:
  - ➤ The size of the recessionary gap, and
  - ➤ The size of the *spending or tax multiplier*

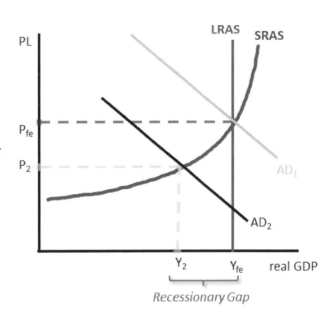

Determining the size of a tax cut or of an increase government spending needed to move an economy in recession back towards is full employment level depends on the size of the recessionary gap and the size of the spending or tax multiplier

Study the graph:
- The economy is producing a level of output $500 million below its full employment level.
- Assume the marginal propensity to consume (MPC) equals 0.75

The government wishes to stimulate spending by enough to return the economy to full employment
1. How much would government spending have to increase by to increase AD back to full employment?
2. How much would the government have to reduce taxes by to increase AD back to full employment?

$$Spending\ Multiplier = \frac{1}{1-MPC}$$

$$Tax \; multiplier = \frac{-MPC}{MRL \; (or \; MPS)}$$

Expansionary Fiscal Policy - Tax Cuts versus Spending Increases

With a $500 million gap between its current output and its full employment output, and with an MPC of 0.75:

1. How much would government spending have to increase by to increase AD by $500 million?

$$Spending \; Multiplier = \frac{1}{1 - MPC} = \frac{1}{1 - 0.75} = 4$$

*   Desired change in total spending = $500 million.
*   Needed change in government spending $= \frac{desired \; change \; in \; AD}{the \; spending \; multiplier} = \frac{500 \, m}{4} =$ **$125 million**
*   *A $125 million increase in government spending should stimulate total demand in the economy by $500 million and shift AD back to its full employment level*

2. How much would the government have to reduce taxes by to increase AD by $500 million?

$$Tax \; multiplier = \frac{-MPC}{MRL \; (or \; MPS)} = \frac{-0.75}{0.25} = -3$$

*   Desired change in total spending = $500 million
*   Needed change in taxes $= \frac{desired \; change \; in \; AD}{the \; tax \; multiplier} = \frac{500 \, m}{-3} = $ **−$167 million**
*   *A $167 million decrease in taxes is needed to stimulate total demand by $500 million*

Expansionary Fiscal Policy – Impact on Deficits and Debt

As we showed above, determining the necessary size of a *fiscal stimulus* (as expansionary fiscal policy is sometimes referred to) requires the use of the spending and the tax multipliers (learned in chapter 3). Note the following:

To achieve a particular increase in AD, taxes would have to be CUT by more than spending would have to INCREASE. There is a reason for this:
*   A tax cut is an INDIRECT injection into the nation's economy.
    *   A tax cut increases the disposable incomes of households
    *   Higher disposable incomes lead to more consumption, but also increase savings and imports, both leakages.
    *   The actual increase in spending, therefore, is less than if the government were to increase AD directly through new government spending.
*   Fiscal stimulus (both tax cuts and spending increases) lead to a budget deficit
    *   Assuming a government started with a balanced budget, if it wanted to stimulate AD, the government would have to incur a deficit.

> ➤ A tax cut will require the government incurs a LARGER deficit in order to stimulate AD by a certain amount than a spending increase.

Expansionary Fiscal Policy – Understanding the effect

Once an expansionary fiscal policy has been undertaken, its impact on the economy can be understood as follows:

- After an increase in government expenditures: Government may spend more on current expenditures or capital expenditures.
  - ➤ The effect is that households see more employment opportunities as the government demands more goods and services.
  - ➤ There is an immediate increase in AD by the amount of increased government spending, but then household consumption and investment by firms increase as well, since there is greater income and more demand in the economy
  - ➤ The ultimate increase in AD is thereby *multiplied* by a factor determined by the proportion of the initial change in incomes that led to further consumption (the MPC)
- After a tax cut: Governments may reduce the level of taxes, or offer tax refunds, to households and businesses.
  - ➤ The private sector sees its disposable income increase, leading to more consumption and investment, but...
  - ➤ Some of the tax cut will be 'leaked' as increases savings and investment.
  - ➤ The increase in AD will be *multiplied* by a factor determined by the MPC. But the *tax multiplier* will always be less than the *spending multiplier* due to the leakage that results from a tax cut.

Expansionary Fiscal Policy – Illustrating the effect

The impact of a tax cut or increase in government spending can be illustrated as follows

- On AD: AD increases by an amount determined by the initial change in spending from AD1 to AD2, and then ultimately to AD3 depending on the size of the multiplier
- On real GDP (output): Output increases as the total demand in the economy increases. Firms respond to growing demand by producing more output.
- On employment: In order to increase their output in the short-run, firms must hire more workers, reducing unemployment in the economy
- On the price level: The increase in total spending increases the scarcity of output and resources, causing *demand-pull inflation*.

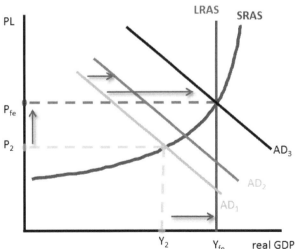

Expansionary Fiscal Policy – When the Economy's at Full Employment

What if a government implements an expansionary fiscal policy when the economy is already producing at its full employment level?

An increase in AD when the economy is already at full employment will cause:

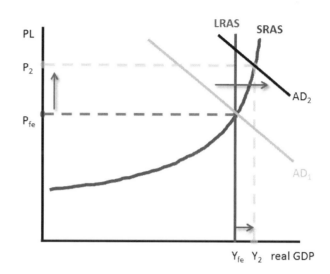

- Only a slight increase in total output:
  - ➤ The nation's resources are already fully employed
  - ➤ Firms are unable to hire the workers they need to meet growing demand
- A significant increase in the average price level:
  - ➤ The economy is now producing beyond full employment
  - ➤ Demand-pull inflation results

Fiscal policy alone cannot lead to long-run economic growth, since it is first and foremost a 'demand-side' policy. Growth requires an increase in AS and AD.

The Role of Fiscal Policy – To Combat Inflation

If an economy is experiencing abnormally high inflation as a result of an increase in AD beyond the full employment level, *contractionary fiscal policy* can be used to reduce AD and bring inflation under control.

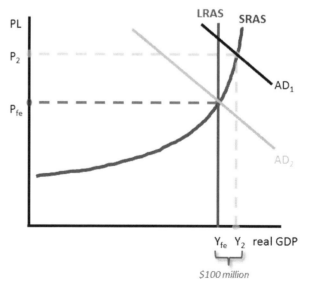

The economy seen here is experiencing an *inflationary gap* of $100 billion.

- Inflation is higher than desired and output is beyond the full employment level
- The government can bring AD down by using *contractionary fiscal policy.*
  - ➤ An increase in taxes on households and firms, or
  - ➤ A decrease in government expenditures
- Either of these policies will reduce total spending, income and employment, and the average price level.

Contractionary Fiscal Policy – Illustrating the effects
The multiplier effects described on an earlier slide works in the opposite direction as well.
- Assume the MPC is 0.75, the spending multiplier is 4 and the tax multiplier is -3.

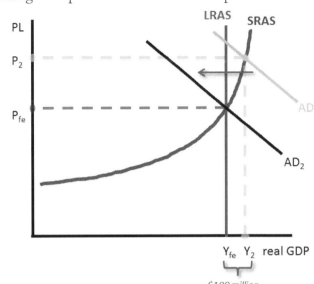

To reduce a $100 million inflationary gap:
- Increase taxes:
  - ➤ A tax increase of $33.3 million will lead to a decrease in total spending of 33.3*-3 = $100 million.
  - ➤ Disposable incomes will fall, consumption and investment will decrease and AD will shift left, reducing the inflationary pressure
- Reduce government spending:
  - ➤ A decrease in government spending of $25 million will reduce total spending by 25*4= $100 million.
  - ➤ Employment and income will fall, putting downward pressure on the price level and moving output closer to the full employment level

Automatic Stabilizers and Fiscal Policy
Not all changes to fiscal policy require explicit action by the government. In most economies, changes to the level of taxation and the level of government spending happen *automatically*. Study the graph below.

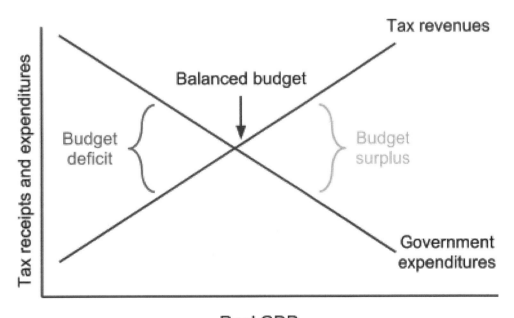

When output falls:
- Tax revenues *automatically decrease:*
  - ➤ Incomes and revenues decrease when AD decreases
  - ➤ At lower incomes levels, households pay lower tax rates
- Government spending increases *automatically:*
  - ➤ More households receive government welfare payments.
  - ➤ More workers receive government unemployment benefits

When output increases:
- Tax revenues increase because households' incomes and firms revenues increase. Some households move up to higher tax brackets and pay higher rates.
- Government spending decreases because fewer households depend on government support.

Fiscal Policy and Long-run Economic Growth

Recall that economic growth, defined as an increase in total output over time, is only possible in the long-run if both AD and AS increase. Therefore, *demand-side* fiscal policies alone cannot produce economic growth. However, some fiscal policies can have positive *supply-side effect* as well.

Supply-side effects of fiscal policy: Certain types of government spending and tax policies can promote increases in aggregate supply, and thereby contribute to long-run economic growth:
- Infrastructure spending: When government supports a modern infrastructure, including for transportation and communications, the private sector is given the resources it needs to grow and succeed in the long-run
- Education spending: *Human capital* is perhaps the most important resource a nation requires for long-run economic growth. Public, government funded schools and programs to improve skills in the labor market can contribute to long-run growth.
- Research and development: Government-funded research and development can lead to scientific, technological, and medical breakthroughs that may spur new industries and promote growth across the private sector.
- Incentives for private investment: Creating a tax policy that rewards innovation and entrepreneurship, rather than punishes it by taxing the 'winners' in an economy will encourage private businesses to invest and thereby help the economy grow.

Fiscal policy is an effective tool for managing AD in the short-run to help maintain price stability and low-unemployment, but *demand-side* policies alone cannot produce long-run economic growth, which requires an increase in both AD and AS. However, some fiscal policies can have positive *supply-side effects* as well.

Fiscal Policy's positive supply-side effects	
Infrastructure spending:	When government supports a modern infrastructure, including for transportation and communications, the private sector is given the resources it needs to grow and succeed in the long-run
Education spending:	*Human capital* is perhaps the most important resource a nation requires for long-run economic growth. Public, government funded schools and programs to improve skills in the labor can contribute to long-run growth.
Research and development:	Government-funded research and development can lead to scientific, technological, and medical breakthroughs that may spur new industries and promote growth across the private sector.
Incentives for private investment:	Creating a tax policy that rewards innovation and entrepreneurship, rather than punishes it by taking the 'winners' in an economy will encourage private businesses to invest and thereby help the economy grow.

Fiscal Policy and the Crowding-out Effect
The use of fiscal policy in times of recession is highly controversial. Opponents argue that an increase in the size of the government during recessions will *crowd-out* private spending in the economy, reducing an economy's ability to *self-correct* from the recession, and potentially reducing the economy's long-run economic growth rate.

Expansionary fiscal policy's effect on the interest rate: Fiscal stimulus requires that a government increases its deficit. This means the government must borrow money in order to stimulate AD. Government borrowing is done using *government bonds*.
- Government bonds: These are *certificates of debt* that a government sells in order to borrow money to finance an expansionary fiscal policy.
- The cost of borrowing: When a government has a history of balanced budgets, investors will be willing to lend it money at very low interest rates, therefore the government does not need to offer a high rate of interest on its bonds. *Fiscally responsible nations can borrow money cheaply.* But if a government has a history of large deficits, investors will demand a higher rate of interest in order to lend it money.
- Crowding-out: *The increase in interest rates that often accompany a deficit-financed fiscal stimulus may cause private investment and consumption in the economy to decrease. Therefore, any increase in AD from new government spending may be off-set by a decrease in private spending, which is crowded-out by higher borrowing costs.*

Illustrating the Crowding-out Effect

Interest rates paid by private borrowers in a nation are a primary determinant of the levels of savings, investment, and consumption. The market in which private interest rates is illustrated is called *the loanable funds market.*

The Loanable Funds Market: A nation's loanable funds market represents the money in commercial banks that is available to be loaned out to firms and households to finance private investment and consumption.

- The price of loanable funds is the real interest rate
- The market shows relationships between real returns on savings and real price of borrowing and the private sector's willingness to save and invest.
- The supply curve represents household savings
  - ➤ At higher interest rates, households save more
  - ➤ At lower rates, households save less
- The demand curve represents investment
  - ➤ At higher interest rates, firms invest less
  - ➤ At lower interest rates, firms invest more

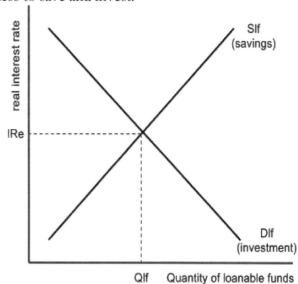

When a government borrows in order to finance a budget deficit, it must increase the interest rates on its bonds in order to attract more lenders.

- Higher rates on government debt will lead households to *take their savings out of private banks* and lend it to government instead
- This causes the supply of loanable funds to decrease, leading to higher borrowing costs in the private sector.
- Before the expansionary fiscal policy, the level investment was Qpr.
- Higher interest rates on government bonds cause the supply of loanable funds to decrease to S1.
- Less money in banks leads to higher interest rates. The quantity funds demanded for private investment falls to Qp.
- Overall spending increases to Qg, but there is a decrease in private investment of Qp-Qpr

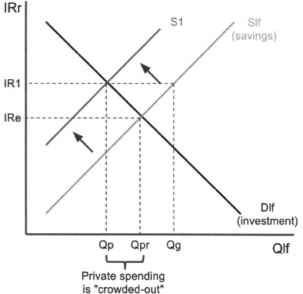

- *Private sector spending is 'crowded-out' by the government's deficit spending. This means AD will not increase by as much as the spending multiplier would predict.*

Illustrating the Crowding-out Effect in the AD/AS Model

Say a government increases spending by $100 million, without raising taxes. This money must be borrowed. Assume the multiplier is 4.

The fiscal policy should lead to an increase in AD of $400 million. However…

- If the government's borrowing reduces the supply of funds available to the private sector, then higher interest rates might cause private investment to fall, therefore,
- The total increase in AD will be less than that which was predicted by the multiplier.
    - To reach full employment, AD would have to increase to AD1.
    - But due to crowding-out, it only increases to AD2.

A much larger stimulus would be needed than the multiplier predicts, further increasing national debt!

Evaluating the Crowding-out Effect

Whether crowding-out will actually occur depends primarily on the depth of the recession the economy was in when the government undertook its expansionary fiscal policy.

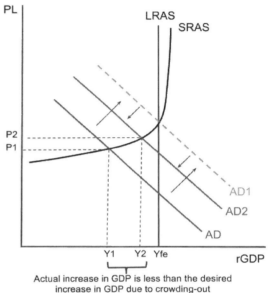

Actual increase in GDP is less than the desired increase in GDP due to crowding-out

During deep recessions: Crowding-out is *unlikely to occur;* private sector investment is already deeply depressed. There is very little spending *to crowd out*, and government should be able to borrow without raising interest rates by much

During mild recessions: Crowding-out is *more likely to occur;* resources are close to being fully-employed, and private sector spending is relatively high. Government will have to offer higher rates to attract lenders, which could cause private investment to fall

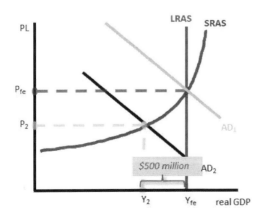

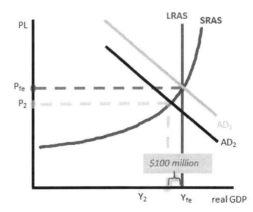

Chapter 6 – Monetary and Supply-side Policies

Interest Rates
- Interest rate determination and the role of a central bank

The Role of Monetary Policy
- The tools of monetary policy
- Monetary policy and short-term demand management
- Monetary policy and inflation targeting
- Evaluation of monetary policy

Supply-side policies
- The role of supply-side policies
- Supply-side policies and the economy
- Interventionist supply-side policies
- Investments in human capital
- Investments in new technology
- Investments in infrastructure
- Market-based supply-side policies
- Labor market reforms
- Evaluation of supply-side policies

Introduction to Monetary Policy

We have already examined the government's use of taxation and government spending as a means of stimulating or contracting aggregate demand to promote macroeconomic objectives. In this chapter we will study an entirely different set of tools policymakers can employ to promote the same macroeconomic goals:

Monetary Policy: A central bank's manipulation of the money supply and interest rates in an economy aimed at stimulating or contracting aggregate demand to promote the achievement of the macroeconomic objectives of
- Full employment
- Economic growth, and most importantly to monetary policymakers,
- Price level stability

What is a Central Bank? A central bank is the institution in most modern, market economies that controls the overall supply of money in the nation's economy. Most central banks act *independently* of the nation's government, and are thus, in theory, insulated from political agendas and influence. Examples include:
- In the US: The Federal Reserve Bank
- In the UK: The Bank of England
- In China: The People's Bank of China

The Role of a Central Bank

Every major world economy has a central bank. Below is a snapshot of one CB and the roles it plays in the nation's banking system and wider economy

The Federal Reserve Bank of the United States	
Overview of the Federal Reserve Bank of the United States	• 12 banks located in different regions of the country • Coordinated by the Fed's Board of Governors • Bankers' banks: Provide banking services to commercial banks ➢ Accept deposits, lends money (called the "discount window", only if commercial banks can't borrow from one another would they borrow from the Fed), issues new currency to private banks • FOMC - Federal Open Market Committee: 12 individuals, including the Chairman of the Fed (Bernanke). Purpose is to buy and sell government securities to control the nation's money supply and influence interest rates. Execute monetary policy.
Functions of the Federal Reserve Bank	• Issue currency: the Fed can inject new currency into the money supply by issuing Federal Reserve Notes (dollars) to commercial banks to be loaned out to the public. • Setting reserve requirements: this is the fraction of checking account balances that commercial banks must keep in their vaults. The larger the reserve requirement, the less money commercial banks can loan out. • Lending money to banks: The Fed charges commercial banks interest on loans, this is called the "discount rate". • Controlling the money supply: this in turn enables the Fed to influence interest rates.

The Money Supply

Money, as measured by economist, is defined as *anything that is widely accepted as payment for goods and services*. Besides being used to buy stuff, money plays other important roles in a market economy.

The Functions of Money: Money serves several important functions in a modern economy.

- Unit of Account: Money can be used to communicate the relative value of different goods and services. For example, a car worth $50,000 is probably of much better quality than one worth $10,000. The money is used as a *unit of account*.
- Store of Value: Money can be saved and spent in the future. The ability of money to store value (in the same way that gold or oil stores value) depends on its continued scarcity over time. If a certain type of money becomes *less scarce* (i.e. there's too much of it in circulation), its loses its value and ceases to function as a strong form of money
- Medium of Exchange: This is the function of money we are all familiar with; it can be used to *buy stuff*. Before money was invented, the only way humans could exchange with one another was through *barter (e.g. trading one good or service for another)*. Money simply makes exchanges easier than they would be without it.

The supply of money in a nation consists of more than just the bills and coins in people's wallets, and there are *less-liquid* (i.e. immediately spendable) forms of money that are also part of the total money supply in an economy.

	Types of Money, from *most liquid to least liquid*
M1	Currency and checkable deposits, this is the most liquid form of money, what can be spent NOW • All paper currency and coins placed in circulation by the central bank. • Money in *checking accounts is* included in M1, since it can be spent almost as readily as currency and can easily be changed into currency. • Excluded from M1 is currency and checking deposits held on reserve by the Central Bank
M2	M2 = M1 + some less liquid forms of money, including: • Savings deposits and money market deposit accounts. • Long-term deposits which can only be withdrawn after a certain period of time
M3	M3 = M1+M2 + less liquid forms of money, including: • Long-time deposits that require substantial penalties to withdraw before maturity • Money market mutual funds, which include money invested in long-term government bonds and other relatively illiquid investments
	When we refer to the 'money supply' we are usually talking primarily about M1

The Demand for Money and Interest Rates

Money, like other assets, has a price. The price of money is the *interest rate*. Interest rates communicate two important pieces of information to savers and borrowers

- To potential savers: The interest rate is the *opportunity cost of holding money as an asset*. If a households chooses to keep cash as an asset itself, what that households *gives up* is the interest rate the money could be earning in a bank. The interest rate is the *price of holding onto money*
  - ➢ *At higher interest rates, the opportunity cost of holding money increases so the quantity demanded of money as an asset decreases as more households will wish to save their money in banks and other institutions that offer a return on the investment*
  - ➢ *At lower interest rates, the opportunity cost of holding money decreases and the quantity of money demanded as an asset increases.*

- To potential borrowers: The interest rate is the *cost of borrowing money*. When a household or firm considers borrowing money to invest in a home or in capital, the interest rate is the *percentage above and beyond the amount borrowed that must be repaid*. It is the 'price of money'.

➢ At higher interest rates, the quantity demanded of money for by borrowers is lower since the cost of repaying the money borrowed is greater.
➢ At lower interest rates, the quantity of money demanded by borrowers is greater because it is cheaper to pay back.

The Demand for Money is inversely related to the interest rate, thus slopes downwards

The Money Market
Since the interest rate is the 'price of money' and we have determined that there is also a supply of and demand for money in a nation, we can illustrate a *money market* by putting these variables together in a graph

Money Supply:
- The supply of money (Sm) is vertical and determined by the monetary policies of the Central Bank.
- Sm is perfectly inelastic, because central bankers to not *respond to changes in the interest rate*, rather they *set the interest rate* by controlling the money supply

Money Demand:
- Money demand (Dm) slopes downwards because at lower interest rates, households and firms demand more money as an asset and for transactions.
- Dm will SHIFT if there is a change in the total output of the nation. At higher levels of output, more money is demanded (Dm shifts right), and at lower levels of output, less money is demanded (Dm shifts left)

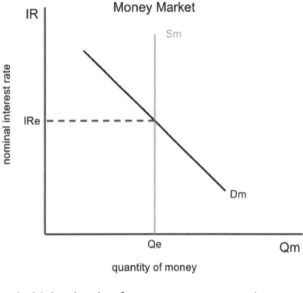

The Money Market – Changes in the Demand for Money:
The demand for money is *inversely related to the interest rate*. A change in the interest rate will therefore cause a *movement along* the money demand curve. But if national output and income change (GDP), the entire money demand curve will shift

Increase in the Demand for Money:
- If the nation's GDP rises, more money is demanded since households are earning higher incomes and wish to consume

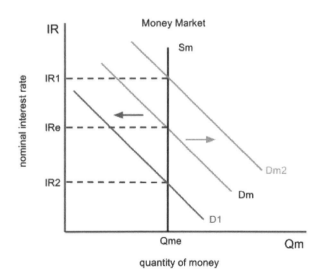

more stuff.

- An increase in demand for money (to Dm2), *ceteris paribus* makes it more scarce. Banks find they must raise interest rates as money demand rises.

Decrease in the Demand for Money:

- If a nation goes into a recession, less money will be demanded since there is more unemployment, fewer workers to pay, and less demand for goods and services
- Dm will shift left (to D1) and money becomes less scarce. Banks will lower interest rates to try and keep borrowers coming through the doors

The Money Market – Changes in the Money Supply
If the supply of money changes, the equilibrium interest rate will change in the economy. Money supply changes result from *monetary policy* actions taken by the central bank.

Increase in the Money Supply:

- An action by the central bank which causes the money supply to increase (from Sm to Sm2) will cause interest rates to fall
- Banks have more money in their reserves, which they wish to loan out, so they will lower the rates they charge to attract more borrowers. *Money becomes less scarce.*
- *Known as an expansionary monetary policy*

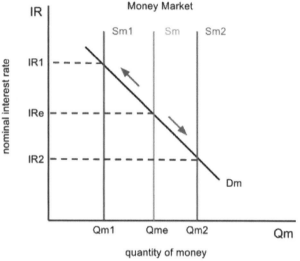

Decrease in the Money Supply:

- An action by the central bank which causes the money supply to decrease (from Sm to Sm1) will cause interest rates to rise.
- Banks have less money in their reserves; therefore have less to loan out. Money becomes *scarcer* and thus the cost of borrowing it rises.
- *Known as a contractionary monetary policy*

Monetary Policy and Aggregate Demand
As we have seen, a change in the supply of money (which is determined by the Central Bank) will directly influence interest rates. But how do interest rates affect the level of aggregate demand? Two of the components of AD are *interest sensitive*, meaning they will change when the interest rate changes.

- Consumption and interest rates: At higher interest rates, the level of consumption will fall because households will prefer to save their money rather than spend it. Also, some types of consumption is often financed with borrowed money (cars, durable goods, and so on), so at higher rates the cost of borrowing is greater and households will chose to consume less
- Investment and interest rates: At higher rates, firms will choose to undertake fewer investments in new capital, since the expected rate of return on an investment is less likely to exceed the borrowing cost the higher the interest rate.

The demand for funds for investment and consumption is inversely related to the interest rate, therefore, higher interest rates will CONTRACT aggregate demand and lower interest rates will EXPAND aggregate demand

Expansionary Monetary Policy
Assume an economy is experiencing a demand-deficient recession. Unemployment is greater than the natural rate, there is deflation, and output is below the full employment level.

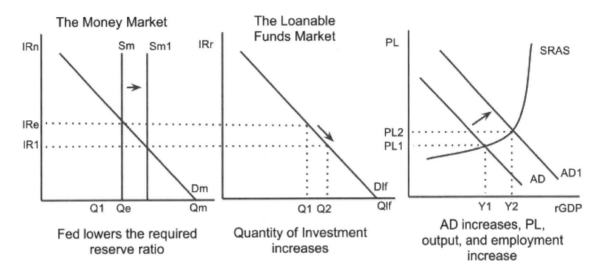

Assume the US Federal Reserve Bank increases the money supply:
- *As you can see above, an increase in the money supply will lead to lower interest rates,*
- *which will lead to an increase in the quantity demanded of funds for investment and consumption,*
- *stimulating AD and moving the economy back to full employment*

Contractionary Monetary Policy
Assume an economy is producing beyond its full employment level, meaning inflation is undesirably high, unemployment is below its natural rate, and the economy is overheating

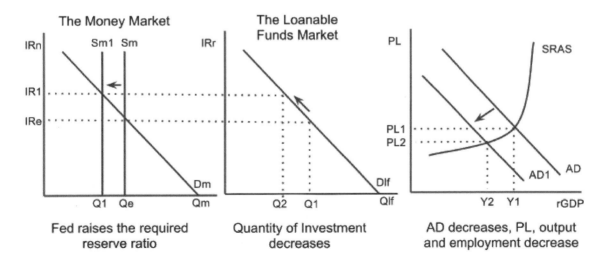

Assume the US Federal Reserve Bank decreases the money supply:
- *A decrease in the supply of money will lead to higher interest rates,*
- *which will lead to a decrease in the quantity of funds demanded for consumption and investment*
- *Reducing AD and moving the economy back to full employment*

Fractional Reserve Banking and Monetary Policy

By accepting deposits from households, then lending out a proportion of those deposits to borrowers, which themselves end up being deposited and lent out again and again, *banks create new money through* their every-day activities.

Required Reserves: Commercial banks are required to keep a certain percentage, determined by the central bank, of their total deposits on reserve at all times. For example:
- A reserve requirement of 20% would mean that a bank with total deposits equaling $1 million would have to keep $200,000 *on reserve* at the central bank. This money may NOT be loaned out by the commercial bank.
- With the other $800,000, the bank can make loans and charge interest on those loans. The bank's business model is to charge a higher interest rate to borrowers than it pays to households saving money with the bank.

Excess reserves: Actual reserves minus required reserves are called excess reserves. This is the proportion of total reserves that a bank is allowed to lend out.

Money Creation: Because banks can lend out their excess reserves banks can actually create new money whenever a deposit is made.

Money Creation in a Fractional Reserve Banking System
Assume that Bank A receives a deposit of $100 and that the central bank requires all commercial banks to keep 20% of their total deposits on reserve (the required reserve ratio [RRR] is 0.2). How can this deposit lead to the *creation of new money* throughout the economy?

The RRR is 0.2. A deposit of $100 into one bank will lead to an increase in checkable deposits across the banking system as follows:

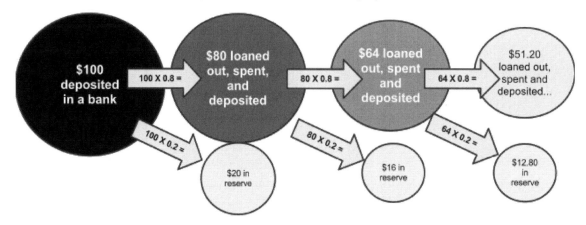

Money deposited in one bank can be loaned out to borrowers, spent, deposited in other banks, and loaned out again. In this way…

An initial change in banks' total deposits will lead to a greater change in the overall money supply in an economy. The degree that the money supply will be affected depends on the size of the MONEY MULTIPLIER

$$The\ Money\ Multiplier = \frac{1}{Required\ Reserve\ Ratio}$$

With the money multiplier in mind, we can determine the total impact on the money supply of a particular change in a bank's checkable deposits. For example, assume an individual deposits $100 in Bank A and the reserve ratio is 0.2

- Bank A will keep $20 on reserve at the central bank
- It will make $80 of new loans, which will be spent, deposited, and 80% loaned out again and again. *The total change in the money supply will be the initial change in Bank A's excess reserves times the money multiplier:* $80 \times \frac{1}{0.2} = 80 \times 5 = \$400$
- *The initial deposit of $100 will lead to $400 of new money throughout the economy*

The Tools of Monetary Policy

Changing the money supply will indirectly expand or contract AD in an economy and allow the central bank to target a particular inflation rate, unemployment rate, or economic growth rate. The tools a central bank has at its disposal to change the money supply are:

- Changing the Required Reserve Ratio (RRR): The percentage of their total deposits commercial banks must keep in reserve. A lower RRR increases the supply of money banks can lend out and leads to a lower interest rate; a higher RRR reduces the supply of money and leads to higher interest rates.
- Changing the Discount Rate: This is the interest rate the central bank charges commercial banks for short-term loans. If this rate is lowered, the supply of money will increase and interest rates will fall. If the discount rate is increased, the money supply will decrease and interest rates will rise.
- Buying or selling government bonds on the open market (open market operations, or OMO): Government bonds (or securities) are held by every major commercial bank in the world.
  - ➢ In addition to lending money to private borrowers (households and firms) banks lend money to governments through purchasing their bonds.
  - ➢ Bonds held by households and commercial banks are highly *illiquid*, meaning they are a form of money that *cannot be spent*.
  - ➢ If a central bank wishes to increase the supply of *liquid money*, it can buy these bonds off of banks and households, increasing the supply of money. If it wishes to decrease the money supply, it can sell these bonds to banks and households

Open Market Operations as a Tool of Monetary Policy

When a central bank buys bonds from commercial banks and households on the open market, the money supply increases by a factor determined by the size of the money multiplier.

Assume the reserve ratio is 0.1 and the Federal Reserve buys $50 million of bonds from commercial banks and the public. *Question: What is the largest possible change in the total money supply resulting from the Fed's open market operation?*

- To answer this question we must first determine the money multiplier: $\frac{1}{RRR} = \frac{1}{0.1} = 10$

- Multiply the *full amount by which the Fed buys bonds* by the money multiplier to find the total change in the money supply: $\$50\ million \times 10 = \$500\ million$

- If a *private individual* deposits a certain amount, you only multiply the *change in the bank's excess reserves* to determine the change in the money supply
  - ➤ If a households deposits $50 in a checking account, the supply of checkable deposits will increase by $50 x 10 = $500. The *money supply*, on the other hand, has only grown by $450, since the initial $50 deposit was already part of the money supply.
  - ➤ When a central bank increases bank deposits through open market bond purchases, the money supply grows by the full amount times the money multiplier, since money held at the central bank was *not previously part of the money supply*.

Expansionary Monetary Policy and the Federal Funds Rate
A central bank's open market operations aim to affect commercial interest rates by targeting the *federal funds rate*.

The Federal Funds Rate: The interest rate that commercial banks charge one another for lending their own excess reserves *to each other* for short-term loans.

To change the federal funds rate:

- The CB can buy bonds from the public, which increases the supply of *federal funds* (as banks now have more funds on reserve at the central bank) from Sf1 to Sf2

- With more funds in reserve, banks charge one another lower interest rates to borrow, a decrease which should be passed on to private borrowers as lower commercial interest rates.

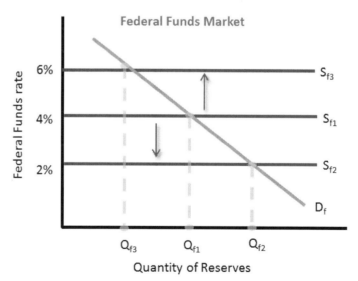

- To increase the FF rate, the CB can sell bonds, reducing the supply of federal funds to Sf3, making them more scarce, raising the rates banks charge each other and private borrowers.

The following example illustrates how a central bank can target the federal funds rate and thus influences commercial interest rates in the economy

- Assume Bank A finds at the end of the day that it has received more deposits than withdrawals, and it now has $1m more in its reserves than it is required to have. Bank A wants to lend that money out as soon as possible to earn interest on it.
- Bank B, on the other hand, received more withdrawals than it did deposits during the day, and is $1m short of its required reserves at day's end. Bank B can borrow Bank A's excess reserves in order to meet its reserve requirement.
- Bank A will not lend it for free, however, and the rate it charges is called the "federal funds" rate, since banks' reserves are held predominantly by the Federal Reserve Bank (in the United States).
- Funds at the regional Federal Reserve Bank ("federal funds") will be transferred from Bank A's account to Bank B's account. Both banks have now met their reserve requirements, and Bank A earns interest on its short-term loan to Bank B.
- *When the CB buys bonds, all banks experience an increase in their reserves, meaning the supply of federal funds increases, lowering the interest rate on federal funds.*
- *Lower interest rates on overnight loans will encourage banks to be more generous in their lending activity, allowing them to lower the prime interest rate (the rate they charge their most credit-worthy borrowers), which in turn should have a downward effect on all other interest rates.*

The Reserve Ratio as a tool of Monetary Policy

Changing the reserve ratio is a powerful way to stimulate or reduce total spending in the economy. It impacts more than just the proportion of deposits banks must keep in reserve.

For example, assume the US Fed wishes to reduce the total amount of money in circulation to increase the interest rate and reduce C and I. By raising the reserve ratio, it can achieve a smaller money supply and a higher interest rate, but also a smaller money multiplier.

	Before the Fed's action	After the Fed's Action
Required Reserve Ratio	0.10	0.15
Money Multiplier	$\frac{1}{0.10} = \mathbf{10}$	$\frac{1}{0.15} = \mathbf{6.67}$

Effect of the Fed's Action:
- With fewer excess reserves to lend out, the money supply decreases and the interest rate rises.
- When new deposits are made, the banks must keep a larger proportion in reserve, reducing the overall money supply in the economy
- For every $1 increase in excess reserves in the future, only $6.67 of new money will be created compared to $10 before the Fed's action.

The Discount Rate as a Tool of Monetary Policy

The discount rate is the interest rate that the Central Bank charges to commercial banks that borrow from the Central Bank

The discount rate's effect on commercial interest rates:

- The Central Bank is "lender of last resort" to commercial banks that have *immediate needs for additional funds (i.e. if at the end of a business day a bank does not have enough in its reserves to meet its reserve requirements, it must borrow from other banks or from the Fed to fulfill this reserve requirement)*
- Commercial banks can temporarily increase their reserves by borrowing from the CB.
- An increase in the discount rate signals that borrowing reserves is more costly and will tend to shrink excess reserves.
- A decrease in the discount rate signals that borrowing reserves will be easier and will tend to expand excess reserves.

The discount rate is a rarely used monetary policy tool. Generally it is kept slightly higher than the federal funds rate, as banks usually prefer to borrow from one another rather than from the central bank

The Relative Importance of the Three Monetary Policy Tools

The three tools of monetary policy are called into action to varying degrees by the world's central banks. The most commonly used tool is open market operations, while reserve ratios and discount rates tend to be changed less frequently.

Relative Importance of the Monetary Policy Tools	
Open Market Operations	Open-market operations is the buying and selling of government bonds in the financial market. Because it is the most flexible, bond holdings by the central bank can be adjusted daily, and have an immediate impact on banks' reserves and the supply of money in the economy
Reserve Ratio	The required reserve ratio is RARELY changed. RRR in the US has been .10 since 1992. Reserves held by the Central Bank earn little or no interest; therefore if RRR is raised, banks' profits suffer dramatically since they have to deposit more of their total reserves with the Fed where they earn almost no interest. Banks prefer to be able to lend out as much of their total reserves as possible
Discount Rate:	Until recently, the discount rate in the US was rarely adjusted on its own, and instead hovered slightly above the federal funds rate. In 2008, the US Fed lowered the discount rate to very low levels as uncertainty among commercial banks brought private lending to a halt. The "discount window" is only supposed to be used in the case of private lenders being unable to acquire funds, hence the Fed is the lender of last resort

Expansionary Monetary Policies

An economy in recession is facing high unemployment and possibly deflation. If the central bank wishes to stimulate aggregate demand, it must increase the money supply. To do this it can:

Reduce the required reserve ratio (RRR):

- Banks immediately see an increase in their excess reserves, giving them more money to loan out
- The money multiplier increases, increasing the money creating ability of the banking system
    - At a RRR of 0.2, the multiplier=$\frac{1}{0.2}=5$
    - At a RRR of 0.1, the multiplier=$\frac{1}{0.1}=10$

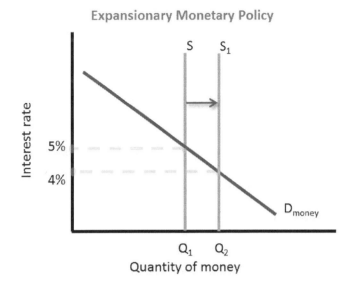

Reduce the Discount Rate:

- Commercial banks can borrow money more cheaply from the central bank, they will be willing to make more loans and borrow from the CB to make up any shortfalls in their required reserves

Buy bonds on the open market:
An open market purchase of government bonds by the CB increases the amount of *liquid money* in the economy and leads to lower interest rates, more spending and more AD

Contractionary Monetary Policies

An economy facing demand-pull inflation with unnaturally low unemployment is over-heating. To bring inflation down, the central bank has the following policy tools at its disposal:

Increase the RRR:

- Banks must call in some of their loans and make fewer loans to meet the higher reserve requirement
- The money multiplier decreases, reducing the money creating ability of the commercial banks.

Raise the Discount Rate:

- Commercial banks now find it more costly to borrower from the central bank. They will be less willing to make loans beyond their excess reserves, since a

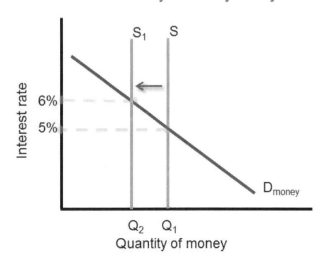

short-fall in required reserves will be more costly to make up with funds borrowed from the CB

Sell bonds on the open market: An open market sale of government bonds by the CB reduces the amount of *liquid money* in the economy and leads to higher interest rates, less spending and a decrease in AD

Evaluating Monetary Policy

To determine the likely effect of a particular monetary policy at stabilizing prices levels or reducing unemployment, several factors must be considered.

Factors that may limit the effectiveness of Monetary Policy	
The degree of inflation:	In periods of extremely high inflation, it is unlikely that a contractionary monetary policy alone will be adequate to bring inflation under control. ➤ The expectation of high inflation creates a strong incentive among households and firms to spend money in the present rather than waiting till the future, when prices are expected to be higher. ➤ A substantial increase in interest rates (to a level higher than the expected inflation rate) would be required to reign in present spending reduce aggregate demand ➤ Contractionary fiscal policy (higher taxes, reduced government spending) may be needed to support higher interest rates during periods of high inflation
The depth of the recession:	In periods of weak demand, high unemployment and deflation, it is unlikely that an expansionary monetary policy alone will be adequate to bring an economy back to full employment ➤ When private spending (consumption and investment) are deeply depressed, a decrease in interest rates may not be enough to stimulate spending and AD ➤ With the expectation of future deflation, the private sector has a strong incentive to save, since money saved now will be worth more in the future. ➤ Expansionary fiscal policy may be needed to reinforce the decrease in interest rates to boost demand to its full employment level.

Evaluating Monetary Policy – Supply-side Effects

While monetary policy is generally considered a *demand-side policy* (since changes in interest rates directly effect investment, a component of AD), it can also have supply-side effects that should be considered.

Consider the economy to the right:

- Assume the central bank lowers interest rates to stimulate AD.
- Lower interest rates lead to more investment and consumption, so AD increases.
- More investment leads to an increase in the nation's capital stock
- More capital makes labor more productive and reduces production costs over time, increasing SRAS and LRAS (to Y_{fe1})

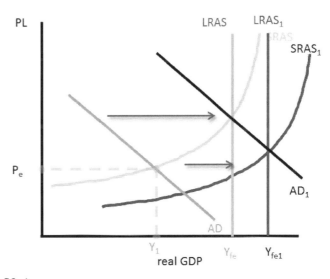

If the economic conditions are right (e.g. firms are willing to invest), expansionary monetary policy can contribute to long-run economic growth!

Introduction to Supply-side Policies

So far we have focused primarily on the *demand-side* fiscal and monetary policies available to government and the central bank to manage the level of economic activity in a nation. Demand-side policies have one major weakness: they are not effective at promoting *long-run economic growth*.

Supply-side policies: Measures undertaken by the government aimed at increasing the level of *aggregate supply* in a nation, and thereby meant to promote long-run economic growth. Examples include:

- Lower business and income taxes
- Elimination of a minimum wage
- Reducing labor union power
- Reducing unemployment benefits
- Deregulation
- Trade liberalization
- Investments in human capital
- Investments in physical capital

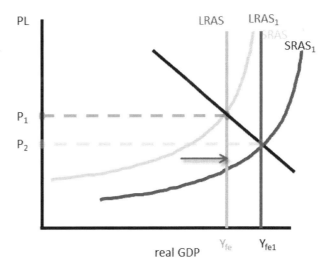

Supply-side policies increase productivity and reduce production costs, shifting AS outwards. Output increases and the average price level decreases

Tax Reform

Reducing business and personal income taxes can positively impact aggregate supply in two ways:

- Business taxes are a cost of production: Lowering taxes on firms reduces the cost of doing business. Allowing business owners to keep a larger share of their earned revenues should incentivize new investments in capital and technology, which increase the productivity of labor and reduce costs, shifting AS outwards.
- Income taxes serve as a disincentive to work: One argument against high marginal income taxes on households goes that *if you tax higher income at higher rates, households have a disincentive to work hard and earn higher incomes.*

  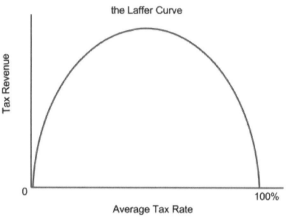

  - ➤ This theory argues that at a certain point, an increase in tax rates will lead to a decrease in tax revenues, if the tax rate is so high that less output is produced.
  - ➤ In contrast, if tax rates are lowered below this level, then tax revenues may actually increase.
  - ➤ The Laffer Curve: Shows the theoretical relationship between the tax rate and tax revenues. Commonly used to support the supply-side argument for lowering taxes

Labor Market Reforms

Labor is the most important (and the most costly) resource for most nations' producers. Reforms of the labor market that bring down the cost of labor will increase a nation's aggregate supply and lead to growth in national output. Supply-side Labor Market Reforms include:

- Reducing or eliminating the minimum wage: The minimum wage is a *price floor in the labor market* set above the free market equilibrium wage rate. Minimum wage laws increase the cost of hiring workers in certain industries (typically the low- skilled sectors). Reducing or eliminating minimum wages may lead firms to hire more workers and thereby produce more output at a lower per unit cost
- Reducing labor union power: Labor unions are organizations of workers in particular industries that negotiate with employers for better worker benefits, such as higher wages, more paid vacation, better health care and so on. Such benefits add to firms' production costs and keep aggregate supply lower than it might be otherwise. Reducing the power of unions will lower labor costs for producers and shift AS outwards.
- Reducing government spending on unemployment benefits: Unemployment benefits are the money payments individuals received during the period of time when they are out of work and seeking a new job. Reducing these benefits would create an incentive for unemployed workers to accept a new job more quickly and at a lower

wage rate than they otherwise might accept. Firms will find more workers willing to work for lower wages.

Deregulation

One of the roles of any government is to regulate the activities of producers in the free market. The goals of regulation are often to reduce the impact of negative externalities arising from the production or consumption of certain goods.

- The cost of complying to government regulation increases firm's average costs and reduces the level of aggregate supply
- Removing or loosening regulations in certain industries will lead to lower costs and greater output, increasing aggregate supply.

Example: The United States Environmental Protection Agency is often accused of imposing harmful regulations on producers of good ranging from automobiles to electricity to agricultural products.

- The benefit of environmental regulations is the reduced emissions of harmful toxins that affect human health and the environment.
- The cost of environmental regulations is the impact they have on employment and the price level. Reducing them will lead to *more output and lower prices* in the regulated industries, *however the tradeoff may be increased environmental degradation and reduced human health*

Trade Liberalization

Free trade refers to the exchange of goods and services between nations *without protectionism by the government.*

Protectionism: The use of tariffs, quotas or other measures aimed at making domestic producers more competitive with foreign producers by limiting the quantity of imports into the nation.

- Tariffs: Taxes place on imported goods, services or resources
- Quotas: A physical limit on the quantity of a good, service or resource that may be imported

The supply-side effects of trade liberalization:

- Reducing protectionism will allow some producers in a nation to import raw materials and other imported factors of production more cheaply, lower their average production costs
- More competition from foreign producers will force domestic firms to use their resources in a more efficient manner, since they will either have to reduce their production costs or lose out to foreign competition.
- Both lower production costs and increased competition lead to an increase in the nation's aggregate supply and contribute to long-run economic growth.

Investments in Human and Physical Capital

Not all investment needed to promote economic growth will be undertaken by the private sector.

Merit and Public goods: There are certain goods that are *under-provided by the free market.*
- Such goods provide social benefits which exceed the benefit to the individual consumer
- They may also be non-excludable, meaning once they are provided, it is difficult for the producer to charge individuals to use them
- For these reasons, such goods will be under-provided by the free market, and therefore if society wishes to have them, it is up to the government to provide them

Education as a merit good: Because the benefits of having an educated population are *social in nature*, it is often up to the government to promote education through public schools.
- ➢ A better educated workforce is more productive, and provides firms with higher skilled workers to produce more and better output
- ➢ A better educated workforce will earn higher incomes and thus pay more in taxes, allowing government to earn more revenues with which it can provide other merit and public goods

Infrastructure as a public good: Due to the fact that is non-excludable, certain types of infrastructure (roads, sanitation, electricity grids, communication infrastructure) may need to be provided by the government
- ➢ Better infrastructure reduces the costs for private businesses and allows them to operate more efficiently
- ➢ Because private firms do not have to build their own roads or railways, they are able to produce and sell their products at lower costs. A modern, efficient infrastructure allows for AS to increase over time.

Evaluation of Supply-side Policies
A policy that increases aggregate supply appears to be overwhelmingly beneficial for a nation's economy.
- The average price level of goods and services decreases, while...
- Output increase, and...
- Employment increases...

However, such policies are often difficult to undertake and may have some undesirable consequences:
- Increased inequality:
  - ➢ Supply-side labor market reforms often result in lower incomes for the working class in a nation, as unemployment benefits, labor union power and minimum wages are all reduced.
  - ➢ Supply-side tax reforms may also redistribute the total burden of taxes in a nation away from the higher income earners and more onto the middle and lower income earners
- Environmental concerns:
  - ➢ Decreased regulation of the private sector may lead firms to find new ways to externalize costs on third parties, often times meaning increased environmental damage
- Political realities:

> ➤ Increasing spending on education and infrastructure is often times politically difficult due to the fact that the payoff from such investments are often not seen for years or even decades, long after the members of the current government are out of office

Chapter 7 – Free Trade and Protectionism

Free Trade
- The benefits of trade
- Absolute and comparative advantage

Restrictions on Free Trade: Protectionism
- Types of trade protection
  - ➢ Tariffs
  - ➢ Quotas
  - ➢ Subsidies
  - ➢ Administrative barriers
- Arguments for and against protectionism (arguments for and against free trade)
  - ➢ Arguments for: protection of domestic jobs, national security, infant industries, protect against dumping, environmental protection, overcoming BoP deficits, source of government revenue
  - ➢ Arguments against: misallocation of resources, threat or retaliation, increased costs, higher prices, reduced competitiveness

Introduction to International Trade

The expansion of voluntary trade between nations has been a defining characteristic of the global economic system since the Second World War. But peoples' views on trade were not always so liberal.

Key Questions about International Trade	
Why do nations trade?	What are the gains from trade between nations?
How does a nation determine what it should produce?	What are the obstacles to free trade?

Specialization based on Comparative Advantage

Because the world's productive resources are not distributed evenly between nations, it does not make sense that every nation tries to produce the same goods. Rather, nations tend to specialize in goods for which their natural, human and capital resources are particularly appropriate to produce. These may be…

Labor-intensive goods		Land-intensive goods	
Examples:	**Where?**	**Examples:**	**Where?**
Textiles Low-skilled manufactured goods	China Latin America Low-wage countries	Agricultural products Minerals Timber resources	North America Russia Australia

Capital-intensive goods	
Examples:	**Where?**
Airplanes	Western Europe
Automobiles	Japan
Microchips	South Korea

What a particular nation should produce and trade is based on what the country has a comparative advantage in the production of.

Comparative Advantage: A country has a comparative advantage in production of a certain product when it can produce that product at a lower relative opportunity cost than another country.

Production Possibilities Analysis of Comparative Advantage

Consider two countries, South Korea and the United States.

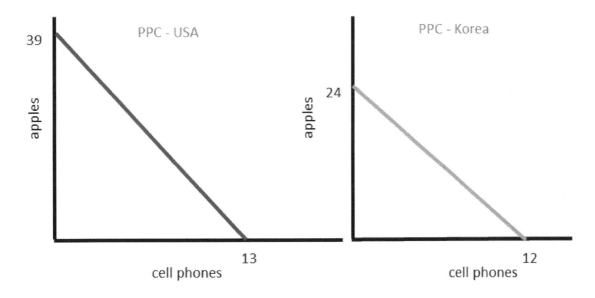

Determining comparative advantage:

How much do apples "cost" each country to produce?

- The US can produce *either* 39 apples *or* 13 cell phones.
- 1 apple = 1/3 cell phone
- S. Korea can produce *either* 24 apples *or* 12 cell phones.
- 1 apple = ½ cell phone

How much do cell phones "cost"?

- The US must give up 3 apples for each cell phone it produces.
- S. Korea must give up only 2 apples for each cell phone it produces.

The US has a comparative advantage in apples, South Korea in cell phones

Because the US has a lower opportunity cost for apples than S. Korea, and S. Korea has a lower opportunity cost for cell phones than the US, these two countries can benefit from specializing and trading with one another.

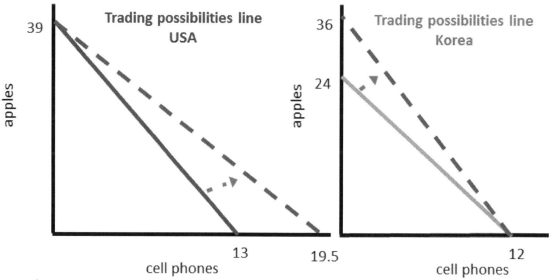

United States:

- Specialize in apples -> trade apples for cell phones with Korea. Korea should be willing to trade 1 apple for anything up to, but not beyond, 1/2 cell phone. Before trade, 1 apple could only get America 1/3 cell phone.
- The US has *gained from trade*.

South Korea:

- Specialize in cell phones -> trade cell phones for apples with the US. The US should be willing to exchange up to three apples for one cell phone. Before trade, Korea could only get two apples for each cell phone it gave up.
- South Korea has *gained from trade*.

The dashed lines represent the maximum amount of output the two countries could hope to consume as a result of trade with one another. This is the trading possibilities line. Trade allows each nation to consume beyond its own production possibilities.

Specialization is defined as *"the use of the resources of an individual, a firm, a region, or a nation to concentrate production on one or a small number of goods and services."*

- What a person, company or country should specialize in depends on the task for which it has the lowest opportunity costs.
- Countries should specialize based on the products for which they have a comparative advantage

Gains from Specialization and Trade
Specialization based on comparative advantage improves global resource allocation.

Specialization and trade based on comparative advantage increases the productivity of a nation's resources and allows for greater total output than would otherwise be possible.

Specialization and Trade based on Production Possibilities Tables
The PPC provides a graphical means of displaying a nation's potential output of two goods. The same information can be shown in a table as well. These tables come in two types, Output and Input tables.

Output table
Given a fixed amount of resources, Mexico and the USA can choose between the following alternatives

	Soybeans	Avocados
Mexico	15	60
USA	30	90

In Mexico:
- Mexico can produce 15 soybeans or 60 avocados.
- For each soybean it produces, Mexico is giving up 60 avocados.
- The cost of EACH soybean, therefore, is 4 avocados (60/15).

1 soybean = 4 avocados
1 avocado = ¼ soybean

In the United States
- The US can produce 30 soybeans or 90 avocados.
- For each soybean it produces, it is giving up 3 avocados.
- The cost of EACH soybean is 3 avocados (90/30).

1 soybean = 3 avocados
1 avocado = 1/3 soybean

The US has a comparative advantage in soybeans and Mexico has a comparative advantage in avocados.

Input table
In order to produce one ton of output, Mexico and the USA must use the following amount of resources. (in acres of land)

	Soybeans	Avocados
Mexico	16	8
USA	8	6

In Mexico:
- To produce 1 ton of soybeans, 16 acres of land must be used.
- On those same 16 acres, Mexico could produce 2 tons of avocados (16/8).
- Each soybean costs Mexico 2 avocados (16/8).

1 soybean = 2 avocados
1 avocado = ½ soybean

In the United States:
- To produce 1 ton of soybeans, 8 acres of land must be used.
- On those same 16 acres, the US could only have produced 1.33 avocados (8/6).
- Each soybean costs the US 1.33 avocados (8/6).

1 soybean = 1.33 avocados
1 avocado = 0.75 soybeans

The US has a comparative advantage in soybeans and Mexico has a comparative advantage in avocados

How to determine specialization and trade based on a production possibilities table
1. Identify the opportunity costs of the two goods in each country
2. The countries should specialize in the good for which they have the lower opportunity cost.
3. The countries should trade with each other to get the good that they are not producing.

Cross-multiplication trick.
For an output problem, simply cross multiply and then choose the highest level of output.

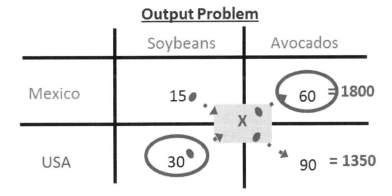

Based on the table above, Mexico has the comparative advantage in avocados and the US in soy beans. The two countries should specialize and trade with one another based on these advantages.

Output is maximized when the US specializes in soybeans and Mexico in avocados.

For an input problem, cross-multiply and then choose the combination that uses the least amount of inputs.

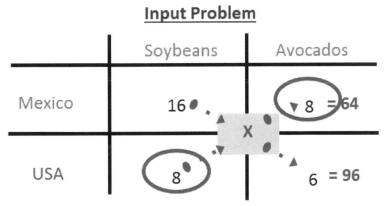

Inputs are minimized when the US specializes in soybeans and Mexico in avocados.

Absolute Advantage versus Comparative Advantage
Having put the data into a PPC, it is clear that the US is, in fact, better at producing BOTH avocados and soybeans. The US has an **absolute advantage** in both goods
- Absolute Advantage: When a nation can produce a certain good more efficiently than another nation.
- How is this different from comparative advantage? Having an absolute advantage in a product, as the US does in both soybeans and avocadoes, does not mean a country has a lower opportunity costs in both products. The US should still only specialize in what it has a *comparative advantage in.*

Soybeans:
> In the US: 1s = 3a
> In Mexico: 1s=4a

Avocados
> In the US: 1a=1/3s
> In Mexico: 1a=1/4s

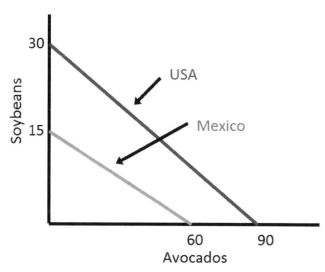

The USA has an *absolute advantage* in both soybeans and avocados, because, given a certain amount of resources, it can *produce more* of both goods.

But Mexico has a *comparative advantage* in avocados, because it has to give up only 1/4 soybean versus America's 1/3 soybean. Mexico's opportunity cost of avocados is lower than America's, therefore both countries could gain from trade if Mexico specialized in avocados and America in soybeans, and trade took place.

The Gains from Trade in a Supply and Demand Diagram
The gains from free trade can be illustrated in a diagram showing the supply and demand of a particular good that is being traded between to nations.

The graph shows the market for cars in the United States under free trade:
- Sd: The domestic supply of cars
- Dd: The domestic demand for cars
- Pd and Qe: Equilibrium price and quantity before free trade
- S_world: The world supply of cars
  > Since the US is just one of nearly two hundred countries buying cars, American consumers can buy as many as they wish without affecting the price, so world supply is perfectly elastic
- Pw: The world price of cars
- Q1: The domestic quantity supplied with trade:
- Q3: The domestic quantity demanded with trade

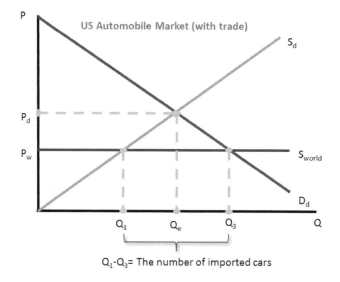

There are winners and losers from free trade in the US automobile market, but overall society is better off than it would be without trade.

The losers from free trade:
- Notice that Q1 is less than Qe. This means that *fewer cars are produced in the US* than would be without trade. Domestic producers suffer due to the lower prices of imported cars. Domestic producer surplus is less than it would be without trade.
- Workers in domestic factories may lose their jobs, as output of American cars declines

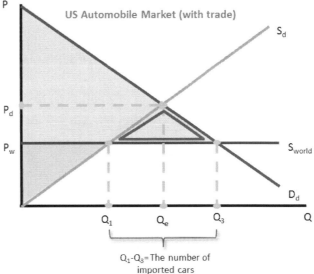

The winners from free trade
- Q3 is greater than Q3, indicating that consumers buy more cars after trade than they would without trade.
- Pw is lower, indicating that consumers enjoy a lower price and more consumer surplus than before trade

Effect of trade on total welfare: Because of free trade, total welfare in the car market has increased by the triangle outlined in gray.

Introduction to Protectionism

Despite the gains from trade we have explained and illustrated using both PPCs and supply and demand diagrams, almost every country still chooses to engage in some degree of *protectionism.*

Protectionism: The use of tariffs, quotas, subsidies or administrative measures aimed at making domestic producers more competitive with foreign producers by limiting the quantity of imports into the nation.
- Tariffs: Taxes place on imported goods, services or resources. A tariff increases the cost of imported goods, reducing their supply and causing the price paid by domestic consumers to rise. Therefore, the domestic quantity supplied is greater than it would be without the tariff.
- Quotas: A physical limit on the quantity of a good, service or resource that may be imported. A quota on a particular good will result in a shortage of imports in the short-run, which drives up the domestic price and leads domestic producers to increase their quantity supplied.
- Protective subsidies: Payments from the government to domestic producers meant to either increase domestic consumption of their goods or to promote the export of their goods to the rest of the world. The subsidy increases the domestic supply of a good and therefore increases the quantity consumed by domestic consumers.

All forms of protectionism lead to a misallocation of society's resources and ultimately reduce total welfare. However, there are several arguments for protectionism that must be evaluated

Protectionist Tariffs

A tariff on an imported good reduces its supply and drives the price up for domestic consumers and producers. Consider the market for cars in the United States once again.

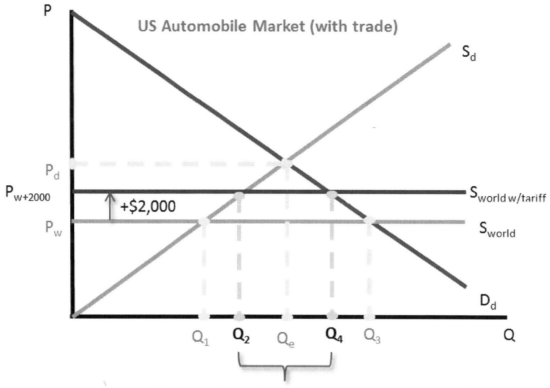

Q_2-Q_4= The number of imported cars after the tariff

Assume the US government places a tariff of $2,000 on all imported cars.
- The world supply shifts *up* by the amount of the tariff. All cars now cost $2000 more
- The domestic quantity supplied increases from Q1 to Q2
- The domestic quantity demanded decreases from Q3 to Q4
- The quantity of cars imported decreases from Q1-Q3 to Q2-Q4

The tariff leads to more cars being produced domestically, but fewer consumed and higher prices for consumers!

Tariffs cause the price of the taxed good to rise and domestic output to increase. But to evaluate the overall effect of the tariff, more factors must be considered.

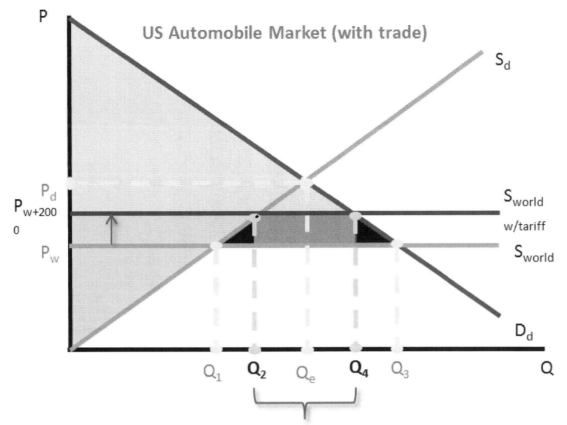

Q₂-Q₄= The number of imported cars after the tariff

Effect of the tariff on all stakeholders
- On consumers: Consumer surplus (the triangle below D_d and above P_{w+200}) is now a smaller area, since the price is higher and quantity lower.
- On domestic producers: Producer surplus is now greater, since domestic producers sell more cars at a higher price
- On foreign producers: Foreign producers are worse off. They sell fewer cars and earn less revenue ($[Q_2-Q_4]*P_w$) than they did before the tariff
- On the government: The government levying the tariff earns revenue equal to the rectangle between Q_2 and Q_4, below P_{w+200} and P_w.
- On total welfare: There is a *net loss of total welfare* equal to the two black triangles. Society as a whole is *worse off* because fewer cars are consumed but the relatively inefficient domestic producers produce more cars.

Protectionist Quotas
A quota is a physical limit on the quantity of a particular good (or goods) that may be imported. Assume that rather than taxing imported cars, the US government places a quota of just 1 million imports per year.

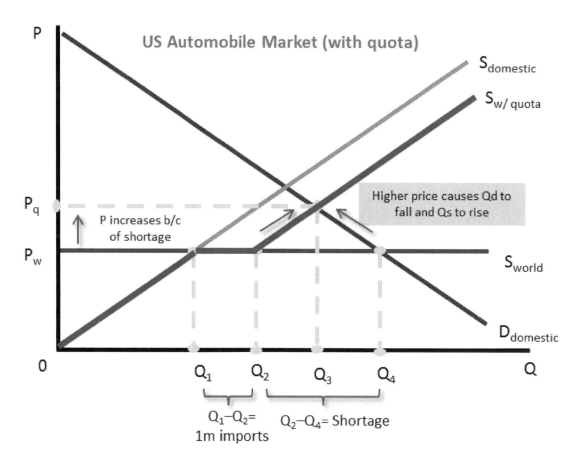

The effects of the quota:

- Before the quota, Q1-Q4 cars were imported. After the quota, only Q1-Q2 cars can be imported.
- The quota creates a shortage at the world price of Q2-Q4 cars.
- Because of the shortage, the price of cars rises from Pw to Pq.
- At the higher price, domestic quantity supplied increases from Q1 to 0-Q1 and Q2-Q3.
- Total quantity demanded at the higher price is Q3, but Q1-Q2 will be imported.

The new domestic supply curve is the bold line

A quota on imported cars caused the price to rise and the domestic quantity supplied to increase. But to determine the net effect of the quota we must examine its effect on various stakeholders.

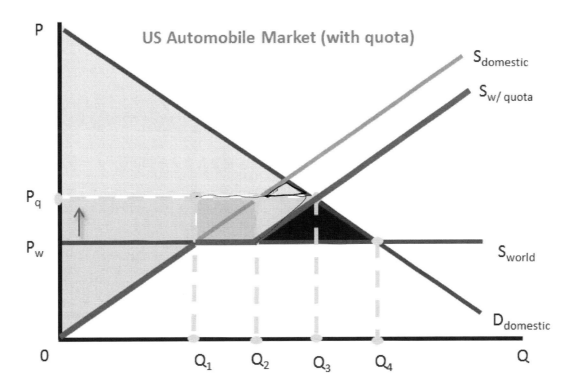

Effect of the quota on all stakeholders

- On consumers: The quantity of cars falls and the price rises, so consumer surplus is reduced to the triangle above P_q and below $D_{domestic}$
- On domestic producers: Output and price have increases, so producer surplus increases to the areas below P_q and above $S_{w/quota}$ between 0 - Q_1 and Q_2 - Q_3
- On foreign producers: There will be fewer imports (only Q_1-Q_2) but they will sell for higher prices, but overall revenues fall for foreign producers.
- On the government: Unlike a tariff, no revenues are collected from a quota.
- On total welfare: Total welfare decreases due to fewer cars being sold and more being produced by relatively inefficient domestic producers. The black triangle is the area of welfare loss

Protectionist Subsidies

A third form of protectionism is government subsidies to domestic producers. Assume the US government provided a $2,000 subsidy to American auto manufacturers for every car produced.

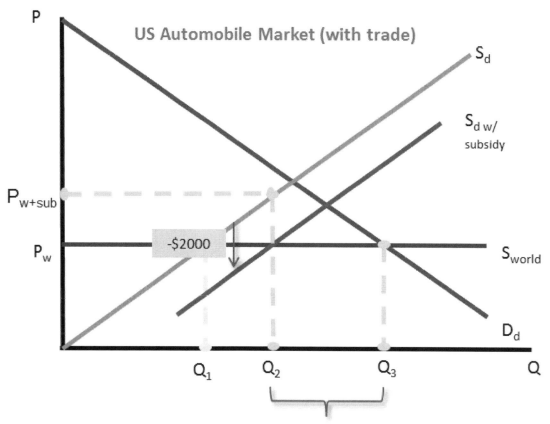

Q_2-Q_3= The number of imports after subsidy

The effects of a protectionist subsidy:

- The domestic supply increases from S_d to $S_{d\,w/\,subsidy}$, a 'downward' shift of $2,000
- The world price is still below the domestic price, so consumers will still pay the price P_w for cars. Producers receive P_{w+sub} (the world price plus the subsidy)
- Because of the increased supply, domestic output will increase from Q_1 to Q_2.
- Imports will decrease from Q_1-Q_3 to Q_2-Q_3.

The subsidy leads to more cars being produced domestically, and fewer cars being imported, making it a form of protectionism

From the analysis above, it appears at first glance that a protectionist subsidy will help domestic producers without harming domestic consumers (who still pay the world price). However, this conclusion is incomplete because it does not include *all stakeholders*.

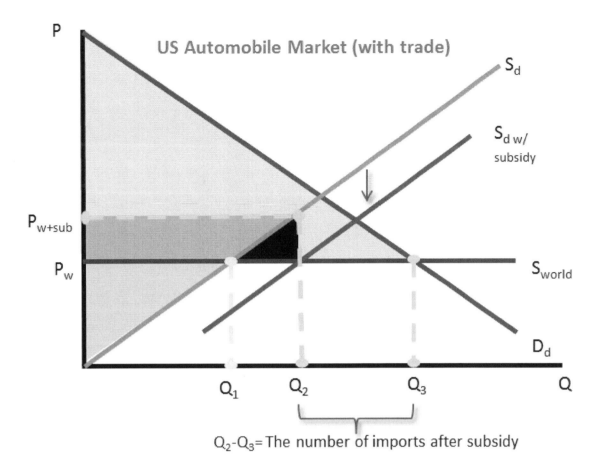

Q_2-Q_3 = The number of imports after subsidy

Effect of a subsidy on all stakeholders

- On car consumers: No effect. The price is still P_w, they still buy Q_3 cars, and consumer surplus equals the area below D_d and above P_w.
- On domestic producers: They receive a higher price (P_{w+sub}) and produce a greater quantity (Q_2) so producer surplus increases to area below P_{w+sub} and above S_d
- On foreign producers: They are clearly worse off; since fewer cars are imported, their revenues fall.
- On taxpayers and the government: The cost of the subsidy to taxpayers (the amount of the subsidy multiplied by the quantity of cars produced) is a rectangle on the graph between P_w and P_{w+sub} and Q_2
- On total welfare: The total cost of the subsidy is greater than the total increase in producer surplus. The black area is the loss of total welfare created by the subsidy.

Calculating the Effects of Protectionist Policies

Up to this point we have analyzed the general effects on consumers, producers, the government and taxpayers and total welfare of protectionist policies. But if we are given linear demand and supply equations, we can actually *calculate* the effects of these policies.

Assume domestic demand and supply of cars in the US are expressed as:

$$Qd = 30,000 - 0.5P \ and \ Qs = -5,000 + 0.75P$$

- Assume the world price of cars is $20,000
  - ➢ *Domestic* $Qd = 30,000 - 0.5(20,000) = 20,000\ cars$
  - ➢ *Domestic* $Qs = -5,000 + 0.75(20,000) = 10,000\ cars$
  - ➢ *Quantity of imports* $= 20,000 - 10,000 = 10,000\ cars$

Now the US government grants a $2,000 per car subsidy to US producers. The new supply equation is:

$$Qs = -5,000 + 0.75(P + 2,000),\ or ... Qs = -3,500 + 075P$$

- At the world price of $20,000, American carmakers will now make:
  - ➢ $Qs = -3,500 + 0.75(20,000) = -3,500 + 15,000 = 11,500\ cars$
  - ➢ *The quantity demanded will still be 20,000 cars since Pw did not change*
  - ➢ *The new quantity of Imports* $= 20,000 - 11,500 = 8,500\ cars$

The effects of the protectionist subsidy can be graphed and calculated using the numbers on the graph. (The figures below are all in thousands):

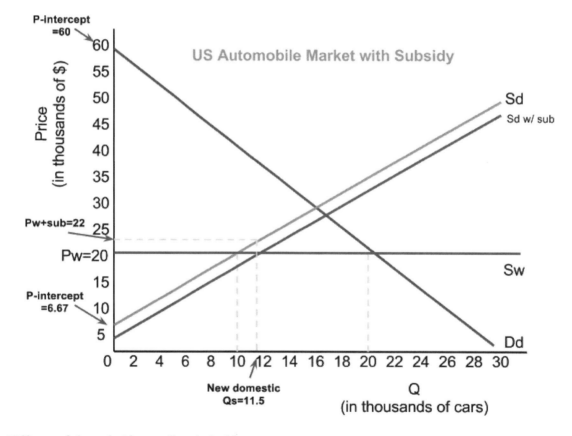

Effects of the subsidy on all stakeholders
- Consumer surplus before and after subsidy: $\frac{(60-20)\times20}{2} = 400$
- Producer surplus:
  - ➢ Before: $\frac{(20-6.67)\times10}{2} = 66.65$
  - ➢ After: $\frac{(22-6.67)\times11.5}{2} = 88.15$

- ➤ Increase: $88.15 - 66.65 = 21.5$
  - Foreign producer revenues:
    - ➤ Before: $10 \times 20 = 200$
    - ➤ After: $8.5 \times 20 = 170$
- Cost to taxpayers of subsidy: $11.5 \times 2 = 23$
- Loss of welfare (the difference between the cost of the subsidy and the increase in producer surplus): $23 - 21.5 = 1.5$

The cost of the subsidy exceeds the benefit, so it has led to a loss of total welfare of $1,500

Other forms of Protectionism

Besides tariffs, quotas and subsidies, there are other forms of protectionist measures a government can take to shelter domestic firms from foreign competition. These include:

Voluntary Export Restraints (VERs): an agreement between two nations to limit trade in particular commodities so that the producers in one nation can remain in business providing commodities to the domestic market, rather than be forced to compete with more efficient foreign producers.

Administrative obstacles: "the red tape" that governments may erect when free trade agreements limit the imposition of tariffs and quotas.

- May include overly burdensome quality controls, safety regulations, living-wage and other workplace standards to be met by foreign producers.
- If foreign producers cannot meet these standards, their products are forbidden from being sold domestically. May include environmental, health and safety standards.

DUMPING: *The act of a manufacturer in one country exporting a product to another country at a price which is either below the price it charges in its home market or is below its costs of production*

Arguments for and Against Protectionism

Protectionism always leads to a *loss of total welfare (or deadweight loss)* for in the protected industries. So why do countries still practice it? Here are some of the arguments for and against protectionism.

Arguments for:	• Protection of domestic employment: More jobs in the export sector • Protection of infant industries: Allows young industries to grow under government protection until they can compete with foreign producers. • To prevent dumping: When foreign producers sell their output at below costs of production in domestic market • To enforce product standards: Protect consumers from low quality, unsafe imports • To raise revenue: Tariffs raise revenue for government, which could go towards providing public goods • To protect strategic industries: Defense, energy food; key industries may be best left to domestic producers

Arguments against:	• Leads to a misallocation of resources: Too much of the protected good will be produced domestically, not enough by relatively efficient foreign producers • Could lead to a trade war: If trading partners retaliate with their own protections, even worse resource allocation will result. • Higher priced imports: In the case of quotas and tariffs consumers suffer from higher prices and some producers will have to pay more for imported raw materials. • Reduced competitiveness: Industries sheltered by protectionism will become less and less competitive over time, requiring even more protection and a greater loss of welfare.

Based on all our analysis, some broad conclusions can be made about most forms of protectionism. Ultimately, protectionism creates some winners and losers, but the cost to the losers exceeds the benefits to the winners. Protectionism...

• Benefits: Domestic producers may benefit b/c they receive a higher price for their output. The federal government may gain through revenue from tariffs.

• Harms: Consumers are harmed because they pay higher prices for goods produced by the protected industry. Foreign producers are hurt because they are not able to sell their as much of their output as they would be able to otherwise, so their profits are reduced.

Most Economists oppose protectionism: In most cases, the costs of protectionism exceed the benefits. Consumers are hurt by the higher prices they pay, while producers often benefit less. Also, industry employs large amounts of economic resources in "rent-seeking" as they lobby congress to erect barriers to trade. In most cases, protectionism results in deadweight loss for society, meaning economic inefficiency.

Chapter 8 – Exchange Rates

Freely Floating Exchange Rates
- Determination of freely floating exchange rates
- Causes of changes in the exchange rate
- The effects of exchange rate changes

Government Intervention in Foreign Exchange Markets
- Fixed exchange rates
- Managed exchange rates (managed float)
- Evaluation of different exchange rate systems

Introduction to Exchange Rates

In international trade it becomes necessary for individuals in different countries who want to buy and sell from one another to exchange currencies. There are approximately 150 different currencies in circulation in the world today. In the process of trading between nations, foreign exchanges of currency must be made.

The Exchange Rate: This is the value of *one currency* expressed in terms of *another currency*. For example:
- The exchange rates of the US dollar in the UK: $1 = £0.65
- The exchange rate of the British pound in the US: £1 = $1.56
  - The British pound is *stronger* than the US dollar
  - *$1 worth of US goods will cost a British consumer only £0.65*
  - *£1 worth of British goods will cost a US consumer $1.56*

Appreciation and depreciation:
- If one currency gets stronger relative to another (its exchange rate increases), the currency has appreciated. Example: The dollar is now worth £0.8; the dollar has appreciated
- If one currency gets weaker relative to another (its exchange rate decreases), the currency has depreciated. Example: The pound is now worth $1.25; the pound has depreciated

The Foreign Exchange Market

Exchange rates, or the "prices of currencies" are determined in a market, just like the price of anything else in a market economy. The market for a currency is known as *the foreign exchange market*, or, more simply, as the *forex market*. Consider the two forex markets below:

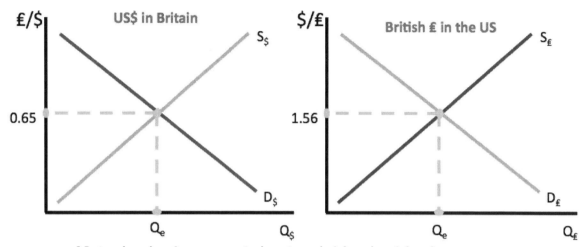

Notice: the value of one currency is the reciprocal of the value of the other currency:

In the market for dollars:
- The exchange rate, or 'price', is the number of pounds per dollar.
- The supply and demand are for dollars

In the market for pounds:
- The exchange rate, or 'price', is the number of dollars per pound.
- The supply and demand are for pounds

Calculating Exchange Rates

Once you know the value of one currency expressed in terms of another, we can easily calculate the value of the other currency expressed in terms of the original. Study the table below.

1 USD	Euro	British Pound	Indian Rupee	Australian $	Canadian $	South African rand	New Zealand $	Japanese Yen	Chinese yuan
1 US $ =	0.81	0.64	55.51	0.95	1	8.23	1.23	78.13	6.36
Inverse:	1.23	1.56	0.02	1.05	1	0.12	0.81	0.013	0.16

- The first row tells us how much one dollar 'costs' in each of the foreign currencies. In other words, it's the dollar exchange rate in Europe, Britain, India, and so on...
- The second row tells us how much the foreign currency costs to Americans. For example,
  - One euro's worth of goods from Germany 'costs' Americans $1.23. 100 euros of output would cost $123.
  - One rand worth of South African output would only cost an American $0.12. But 100 rand of output would cost $12.
  - *The value of one currency is always the inverse of the other currency's value*

Calculating Prices Using Exchange Rates

With knowledge of exchange rates, we can easily calculate how much a good produced abroad in one currency will cost a foreign consumer who is spending another currency. Knowing the exchange rate of the US dollar in the nine countries below, fill in the last row of this table

1 USD	Euro	British Pound	Indian Rupee	Australian $
1 US $ =	0.81	0.64	55.51	0.95
Price of a $1000 American product in each currency	=1000×0.81 =810€	=1000×0.64 =640£	1000×55.51 =5,551r	1000×0.95 =950AU$

- In each case we have simply to multiply the price of the good in US dollars by the exchange rate of the dollar in each country.
- If the dollar were to appreciate, the price of the $1,000 American product would go UP for foreign consumers. This helps explain why America's net exports decrease when the exchange rate rises.
- If the dollar were to depreciate, US products would become cheaper to foreign consumers, which is why net exports will rise when a currency depreciates.

Demand and Supply in the Forex Market

In a particular currency's forex market, both domestic stakeholders and foreign stakeholders play a role. For example, the market for US dollars in Britain:

Supply: American households, firms, banks and the government supply dollars to Britain, so that they can buy British goods, services, financial and real assets

Demand: British households, firms, banks and the British government demand dollars, which they wish to have in order to buy American goods, services, financial and real assets

Note: In the market for pounds in the US, the demand and supply are reversed. Americans demand pounds and British supply them!

121

Recall the laws of demand and supply, which explain why demand slopes downwards and supply slopes upwards. In a forex market, the explanations for these relationships are as follows:

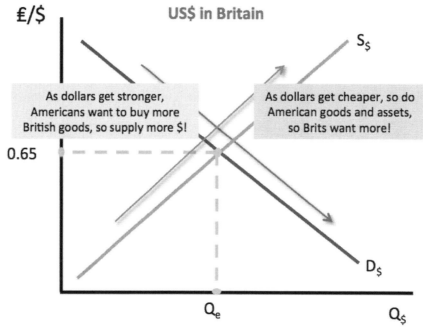

Demand for a currency is inversely related to the currency's value:
- Because as a currency becomes less expensive, so do the goods, services and assets of that country
- Foreign consumers and investors will wish to buy more of the country's goods, services and assets; therefore, they demand greater quantities of the currency as it depreciates.

Supply of a currency is directly related to the currency's value:
- Because as it appreciates, foreign goods become cheaper, so holders of the currency will supply greater quantities in order to buy more foreign goods, services and assets.

Changes in the Exchange Rate
We now know that an exchange rate is determined by supply and demand for a currency. Therefore, if supply or demand change, the exchange rate changes.

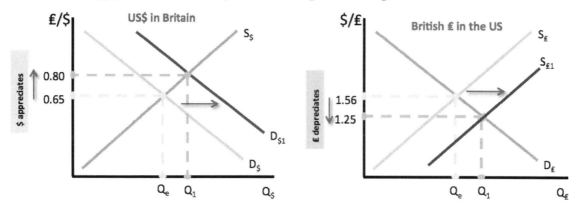

Assume demand for dollars increases in Britain:

- The D$ curve shifts outwards, causing the dollar to become more scarce in Britain. The dollar appreciates.
- In order to buy acquire more dollars, British households, firms, government or banks must supply more pounds. Pounds become less scarce in the US market, and therefore depreciate.
- *An appreciation of one currency is always accompanied by a depreciation of the other currency.*

Exchange Rates Determined from Equations

As with goods in product markets, the demand for and supply of a currency in a foreign exchange market can be expressed using linear equations. From these, we can determine the equilibrium exchange rate and the quantities of the currency that will be traded in a country. Assume the demand and supply for Euros in Switzerland is represented by the equation

$$Qd=100-50E$$

and supply as:

$$Qs=10+30E$$

- The equations express how many *millions of euros would be demanded and supplied at different exchange rates for the euro.*
- *E* is the exchange rates in of euros in Swiss francs (CHF)
  For every 1 CHF increase in the price of a euro, 50 million *fewer* euros will be demanded by Swiss households. This is because European goods are getting *more expensive* and thus Swiss demand less of the European currency.
  For every 1 CHF increase in the value of a euro, Europeans will supply 30 million *more* euros to the Swiss market. This is because Swiss goods are becoming *cheaper* to European households, so Europeans supply more euros in order to buy Swiss goods.

With the supply and demand for Euros in Switzerland known, we can easily calculate the equilibrium exchange rate of the euro in Switzerland.

$$100-50E=10+30E$$
$$90=80E$$
$$E=1.125$$

- One euro 'costs' a Swiss household 1.125 CHF.
- With this exchange rate, we know that:
  A car that costs 20,000€ will cost a Swiss consumer 22,500 CHF.
  A hotel room in Berlin that costs 100 € per night will cost a Swiss guest 125 CHF
- If the euro appreciates, ceteris paribus,
  - Swiss households will demand fewer euros (50 million less for every 1CHF increase in its value). This is because Swiss consumers will demand fewer European goods and services

> ➢ European households will supply more euros to Switzerland (30 million more for every 1CHF increase in value). This is because European consumers will demand more Swiss goods and services, and therefore supply more euros

The supply or demand for a currency may change if one of the determinants of exchange rates changes. This will result in a new equation and a new equilibrium exchange rate. Assume that there is a financial crisis in Europe and Swiss investors wish to hold less European assets. As a result, the demand for euros decreases in Switzerland. At the same time, European investors demand more Swiss assets and therefore the supply of euros in Switzerland increases. The new equations for demand and supply are:

$$Qd=80-50E \text{ and… } Qs=15+40E$$

The new equilibrium exchange rate for the Euro can be calculated

$$80-50E=15+30E$$
$$65=80E$$
$$E=0.8125$$

The euro has *depreciated* against the Swiss franc.
- Because demand for it has fallen while its supply increased, the euro is much less scarce in Switzerland
- European goods can be bought much more cheaply as a result (only 0.8125 CHF must be given for a euro's worth of output instead of 1.125 CHF)

Exchange Rate Systems
An exchange rate can be determined in several ways, depending on the degree of control by the nation's government over the value of its currency:
- Floating exchange rates: When a currency's value against other currencies is determined solely by the market demand for and supply of it in the other countries' forex market. Neither governments nor central banks make any effort to manipulate the value of the currency.
- Fixed exchange rates: When a currency's value against one or more other currencies is set by the government or central bank in order to promote particular macroeconomic objectives. Exchange rate fixing requires governments or central banks to intervene in the forex market to manipulate the demand for or supply of the currency.
- Managed exchange rates: When a currency's value against one or more other currencies is allowed to fluctuate between a certain range by the country's government or central bank. If the exchange rate gets *below a certain level* or *above a certain level*, then the government or central bank will intervene to bring it back within the desired range.

These three exchange rate systems are practiced to varying degrees by different countries at different times, depending on countries' macroeconomic objectives

The Determinants of Floating Exchange Rates

We know that exchange rates are determined by the demand for and supply of currencies. But what determines the demand and supply? There are several determinants of exchange rates

The Determinants of Exchange Rates: If any of the following change, the demand and supply of a currency will change and it will either appreciate or depreciate against other currencies.	
Tastes and preferences	As a country's exports become more popular among international consumers, demand for its currency will increase and supply of other countries currency in its forex market will increase.
Relative interest rates	There is a direct relationship between the interest rates in a country and the value of its currency. At higher interest rates, foreigners will demand more financial assets from the country, and therefore more of the currency.
Relative price levels (or inflation rates)	If a country's inflation rate is high relative to its trading partners, demand for the country's exports will fall and demand for its currency will fall. If inflation is lower at home than abroad, foreigners will demand more of its exports and its currency.
Speculation	If international financial investors *expect a country's currency to appreciate in the future*, demand for it will rise today. If a currency is *expected to depreciate* demand for it will decrease today. Speculation is simply *betting on the future value of an asset or currency.*
Relative Incomes (or growth rates)	As incomes rise abroad, foreigners will demand more of a country's currency. If foreign incomes fall, there will be less demand for a country's exports and its currency. If domestic incomes rise, ceteris paribus, demand for foreign currencies will rise and supply of the foreign currency will increase abroad, as households wish to buy more imports

Consider the market for British pounds in the United States. Any of the following could cause demand for pounds to increase and the pound to appreciate against the dollar.

What could cause demand for pounds to increase?

- Tastes: If British goods became more fashionable in the US
- Interest rates: If the Bank of England (the central bank) increased British interest rates, Americans would with to invest more money in British assets
- Price levels: If US inflation were to increase while British inflation rates remained low, Americans would demand more *relatively cheap* British goods
- Speculation: If investors in the US *expected the pound to get stronger*, the demand for pounds would increase today.
- Income levels: If the economic growth rate in the US rose faster than in Britain, Americans would demand more imported goods and thus would demand more pounds.

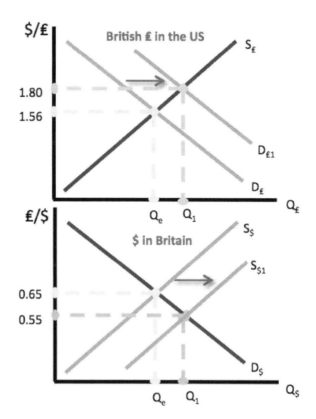

Notice that as the demand for pound increases in the US, the supply of dollars increases in Britain. As the pound appreciates, the dollar depreciates

Introduction to the Balance of Payments

When a currency changes value, there may be several effects on the nation's macroeconomic conditions (employment, growth, inflation) but also on the nation's *balance of payments*

Balance of payments: Measures the flow of money for financial and real transactions between the people of a nation and the rest of the world.

- Current account: Records the flow of money for the purchase of goods and services between a country and its trading partners.
  - ➢ Current account deficit: If a country spends more on imports than it earns from the sale of its exports, its current account is in *deficit* (if M>X)
  - ➢ Current account surplus: If a country earns more from the sale of its exports than it spends on imports, its current account is in *surplus* (if X>M)
- Financial account: Records the flow of money for the acquisition of real and financial assets (factories, office buildings, real estate, government bonds, shares of companies, etc…) by the people of one nation in all other nations.

> ➢ Financial account deficit: If the people of a country owns more financial and real assets abroad than foreigners own of its own assets, its financial account is in *deficit*.

> ➢ Financial account surplus: If the people of foreign countries own more domestic financial and real assets than the country's people own of foreign assets, its financial account is in *surplus*.

Economic Effects of Appreciation and Depreciation

The table below outlines the likely effects on domestic macroeconomic conditions and on a nation's external balance of payments of both an appreciation and a depreciation of its currency

Economic Indicator	Inflation rate	Economic Growth	Unemployment rate	Balance of payments
As a result of appreciation	Inflation will be lower, since imported goods and services and raw materials are now cheaper	Growth will likely slow, since a stronger currency will reduce net exports, a components of AD	Unemployment could rise if net exports decline. Also, domestic firms may choose to move production overseas, where costs are now lower due to strong currency	The current account should move into deficit (since Xn will fall) and the financial account towards surplus, as financial and real assets become more attractive to foreign investors
As a result of depreciation	Inflation will increase, since imports are more expensive, and there could be cost-push inflation if raw material costs rise for producers	Growth should increase, since the country's exports are cheaper and more attractive to foreigners. AD will increase, leading to short-run growth	Unemployment should fall as net exports increase, shifting AD out. Domestic firms may choose to relocate some of their overseas production to the now cheaper domestic market	The current account should move towards surplus (since Xn will increase) and the financial account towards deficit, as financial and real assets become less attractive to foreign investors.

Fixed Exchange Rates

If a government or central bank wishes to *peg* its exchange rate against another currency, it must undertake interventions in the forex markets in order to maintain the desired exchange rate. Consider the market for US dollars in China.

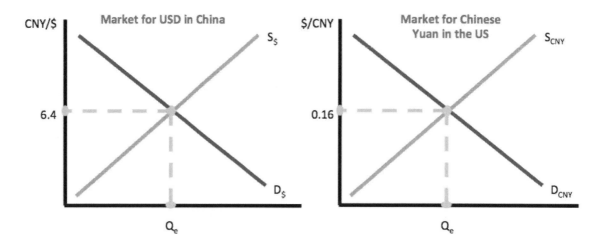

Assume China's government wishes to 'peg' the CNY at 6.4 per dollar (and $0.16 per CNY)

- If the demand for CNY rises, China will have to increase its supply to keep it weak.
- If demand for CNY falls, China will have to intervene to reduce its supply and keep it strong

Methods for maintain a currency peg:	
Interest rates:	The CB can raise or lower interest rates to attempt to change foreign demand for its currency
Official reserves:	The CB can buy or sell foreign currencies to manipulate their supplies and exchange rates
Exchange controls:	The government can place limits on the amount of foreign investment in the country

Assume America's demand for Chinese goods is much higher than China's demand for American goods. This means the supply of US dollars in China is growing faster than demand. Under a floating exchange rate system this would cause the dollar to depreciate in China.

To maintain the dollar at 6.5 CNY:

- The CB can lower Chinese interest rates: Lower interest rates in China would reduce the demand for financial investments in China, reducing demand for CNY in the US and thus supply of $ in China. The dollar would appreciate.
- The CB can print CNY and buy US$ on the forex market:

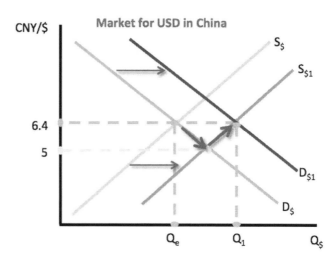

China could increase the supply of CNY in the US by buying up dollars to hold in its foreign exchange reserves; D$ will rise and the dollar will appreciate
- The government can implement stricter exchange controls: By putting strict limits on the amount of foreign currency that can enter China for investments, the supply of US$ would decrease again and the dollar would appreciate.

Managed Exchange Rates

Strict 'pegs' of currencies' values are rather rare these days. More common are interventions by governments and central banks to *manage the exchange rate* of their currency, keeping it within a range that is considered beneficial for the nation's economy. Consider the market for Euros in Switzerland (CHF is for the Swiss franc).

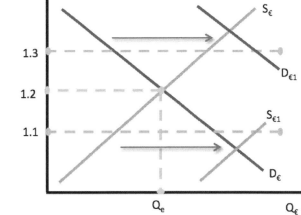

The Swiss National Bank (SNB) wishes to maintain an exchange rate of between 1.1 CHF and 1.3 CHF per euro:

- Assume Europeans wish to save money in Switzerland; the supply of euros increases to $S_{€1}$. To maintain the minimum ER of 1.1 CHF/euro, the SNB must intervene.
  - ➤ *Lower interest rate, buy euros or implement exchange controls to reduce the inflow of euros*
- If Swiss demand for euros grew to $D_{€1}$ the SNB would have to intervene to bring the ER down to the maximum of 1.3 CHF/euro
  - ➤ *Raise Swiss interest rates, sell euros from its foreign exchange reserves, or implement controls on the outflow of CHF*

Evaluating Floating versus Fixed/Managed Exchange Rates

Why might a country's government or central bank choose to intervene in its foreign exchange market? There are several arguments for and against a floating exchange rate system (and therefore against and for managed or fixed exchange rates).

Pros of a floating exchange rate (cons of managed exchange rates):
- Monetary policy freedom: With a floating ER, a central bank may focus its monetary policies on domestic macroeconomic goals. Interest rates may be altered to stimulate and contract AD, rather than to manipulate demand for the currency.
- Automatic adjustment: A floating exchange rate should be the *right* exchange rate, meaning that it reflects the true demand for the nation's currency abroad. Through management, a government may *over-value* or *under-value* its currency on forex markets, which can lead to *persistent deficits or surpluses in the current and financial accounts of the balance of payments.*
- Foreign reserves: A central bank committed to managing its currency's exchange rate must keep large reserves of foreign currencies on hand to intervene in forex markets to manage its exchange rates. This is money earned from export sales that is *not being*

spent on imports, and therefore represents a type of *forced savings* upon the nation's households.

There are also arguments against a floating exchange rate, and for managed or fixed rates.

Cons of a floating exchange rate (pros of managed exchange rates):
- Reduced risk of speculation: A country with a floating exchange rate is vulnerable to speculation by international investors. If investors speculate the country's currency will appreciate, it will likely do so and harm the nation's producers and reduce growth rate. Management prevents such speculative shocks to the exchange rate.
- Inflation control: If a low-income, developing nation has few exports the world demands, it may have a very weak currency, making it expensive to import much needed capital. A government policy that brings up the value of the currency may help make capital goods cheaper and give the country an advantage in its path towards growth and development
- Competitive trade advantage: A country that keeps its currency *artificially weak*, or *under-valued* against other currencies, is likely doing so in order to give its exporters a competitive advantage in international trade. A weak currency contributes to persistent current account surpluses, and keeps employment and economic growth rates high.
- Investor confidence: When less developed countries are seeking foreign investors, a volatile, floating exchange rate may deter potential investment, reducing the country's growth potential. Managed, stable exchange rates may encourage foreign investors to put their money into the economy.

Chapter 9 – Balance of Payments

The Structure of the Balance of Payments
- The meaning of the balance of payments
- The components of the balance of payments accounts
- The relationships between the accounts

Current account deficits
- The relationship between the current account and exchange rates
- Implications of a persistent current account deficit
- Methods to correct a persistent current account deficit
- The Marshall-Lerner condition and the J-curve effect

Current account surpluses
- The relationship between the current account and exchange rates
- Implications of a persistent current account surplus

The Meaning of the Balance of Payments

Through international trade, nations are constantly exchanging goods, services and financial and real assets across national borders. The balance of payments measures the flow of all these transactions.

Balance of payments: Measures the flow of money for financial and real transactions between the households, businesses, banks and government of one nation and all other nations.
- Current account: Records the flow of money for the purchase of goods and services between a country and its trading partners.
  - Current account deficit: If a country spends more on imports than it earns from the sale of its exports, its current account is in *deficit* (if M>X)
  - Current account surplus: If a country earns more from the sale of its exports than it spends on imports, its current account is in *surplus* (if X>M)
- Financial account: Records the flow of money for the acquisition of real and financial assets (factories, office buildings, real estate, government bonds, shares of companies, etc…) by the people of one nation in all other nations.
  - Financial account deficit: If the people of a country owns more financial and real assets abroad than foreigners own of its own assets, its financial account is in *deficit*.
  - Financial account surplus: If the people of foreign countries own more domestic financial and real assets than the country's people own of foreign assets, its financial account is in *surplus*.

The Components of the Current Account

The current account is one of the two primary components of a nation's BoP. The current account measures the balance of trade in goods and services and the flow of income between one nation and all other nations. It also records monetary gifts or grants that flow into our out of a country.

- Goods (the visible balance): This measures the spending by consumers and firms in one nation on another nation's goods (both consumer and capital goods) as well as spending by consumers in the rest of world on the recording nation's goods.
  - ➢ Credits (+): Money earned from exports move a nation's current account balance towards surplus
  - ➢ Debits (-): Money spent on imports move a nation's current account balance towards deficit
- Services (the invisible balance): Services refer to non-tangible purchases such as tourism, banking, consulting, legal services, and transportation. Services can be "imported" and "exported", although there will be no physical transportation of a product involved.
  - ➢ Credits (+): Services provided by a nation but bought by foreigners move the current account balance towards surplus.
  - ➢ Debits (-): Services provided by foreigners and consumed by domestic households move the current account balance towards deficit.

In addition to trade in goods and services, the current account also measures the flow of income and transfers.

- Income balance: The transfer of incomes earned by citizens of one country from activities in another country back to the income earner's country of origin are also measured in the current account. This includes the wage income earned by a country's citizens for employment by foreign companies abroad.
  - ➢ Credits (+): Income earned abroad and sent home moves the current account towards surplus
  - ➢ Debits (-): Income earned at home by foreigners and sent abroad moves the current account towards deficit.
- Transfers balance: A transfer refers to a payment made from one nation to another that is not in exchange for any good or service, such as a gift or a grant. Transfers are divided into two categories, official transfers are payments from one government to another, sometimes known as "aid", and private transfers are payments made by citizens of one country to residents of any other country.
  - ➢ Credits (+): Money transferred from a foreign nation into the home country moves the current account towards surplus.
  - ➢ Debits (-): Money transferred from the home country to foreign countries moves the current account towards deficit.

The Current Account Balance

The sum of the four sub-accounts (goods, services, income and transfers) gives us the current account balance. This can be either:

- In Deficit: When a nation's current account balance is negative. The country spends more on imported goods and services, income and transfers to the rest of the world than it receives in payments for goods and service exports, income and transfers. *Also known as a trade deficit.*
- In Surplus: When a nation's current account balance is positive. The country earns more from its sale of exported goods and services, income and transfers from the

rest of the world than it makes in payments for other countries' exports and income and transfers.

The table below shows the balance on each component of New Zealand's current account, along with the final current account balance, for 2010.

Account	Credits (millions of NZ$)	Debits (millions of NZ$)	Balance (millions of NZ$)
Goods	29,109	-29,706	-597
Services	11,966	-9,777	2,189
Income	2,844	-8,851	-6,007
Current Transfers	1,318	-1,128	190
		Current Account Balance	-4,225

The Components of the Financial Account

The other major account measured in the BoP is the financial account, which measures the exchanges between a nation and the rest of the world involving ownership of financial and real assets.

- Physical assets: Foreigners may buy and sell a country's physical assets, including real estate, factories, office buildings and other factors of production
- Financial investment: International purchases of financial assets, such as shares in companies and government or corporate debt (bonds) bonds are also measured in the financial account
- Capital account: A sub-account of the financial account is the capital account, which measures the transfer of capital goods, money for the purchase of capital goods, and debt forgiveness between one nation and others.
  - ➤ Credits (+): Money transferred by the citizens of foreign countries for investments in physical or real assets, for debt forgiveness or for capital acquisition move the financial account balance towards a surplus
  - ➤ Debits (-): Money transferred from the home country abroad for investments in physical or real assets, for capital acquisition or for debt forgiveness in a foreign country move the financial account balance towards a deficit.

Financial account balance:

- In surplus: If the flow of money *into* a nation's financial account is greater than the flow *out of the country* in a particular year, the country's financial account is in surplus.
- In deficit: If the flow of money out of a country for financial transaction is greater than the flow into the country in a particular year, the country's financial account is in deficit

Official Foreign Exchange Reserves

- If in a given year, the balance of a nation's current and financial account is *not equal to zero*, then the difference will be added or subtracted from the nation's *official reserves of foreign exchange*. Consider New Zealand's current and financial account balances:

Account	Credits (millions of NZ$)	Debits (millions of NZ$)	Balance (millions of NZ$)
Goods	29,109	-29,706	-597
Services	11,966	-9,777	2,189
Income	2,844	-8,851	-6,007
Current Transfers	1,318	-1,128	190
		Current Account Balance	-4,225

Account	Credits (millions of NZ$)	Debits (millions of NZ$)	Balance (millions of NZ$)
Direct Investment	3,895	-1,293	2,602
Portfolio Investment	3,920	-6,947	-3,027
Other Investments	1,272	289	1,561
Capital transfers	1,576	-814	762
		Financial Account Balance	1,898

The change in NZ's official reserves = +$2,327 (this is the amount that will end up in foreign central banks

- A net deficit in the current and financial accounts (as in the case of New Zealand) actually results in an *inflow* (thus, a positive sign) in the official reserves account, since the deficit country must *sell* its reserves of foreign currency to make up for the net deficit.
- If a country has a net balance of payment *surplus,* then the change in the foreign exchange reserves is recorded as a *negative* since the country's ownership of assets denominated in foreign currencies actually increases each year its current an capital accounts added together are positive.

The Balance of Payments

The graphic below provides a summary of the inflows and outflows in a nation's balance of payments.

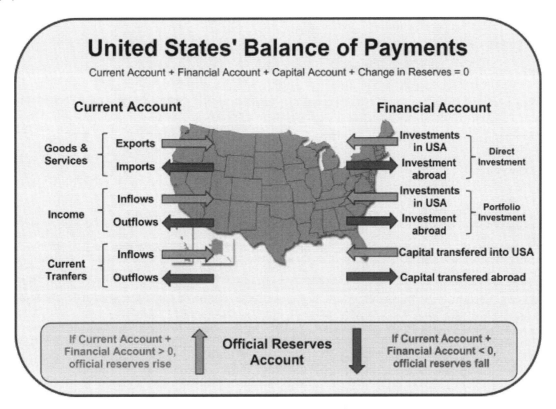

- The arrows pointing inwards indicate money flowing into the country.
- The arrows pointing outwards indicate money flowing out of the country. The total balance of payments must always be equal to ZERO.
  - ➢ A current account deficit will be offset by a financial account surplus
  - ➢ A current account surplus will be offset by a financial account deficit

The sum of all the accounts in the Balance of Payments will equal ZERO: Current account + Financial Account + change in the official reserves

Floating Exchange Rates and the Balance of Payments

Two nations, both with floating exchange rate systems, should, in theory, experience relative balance between their current and financial accounts, experiencing neither deficits nor surpluses. Here's why.

Assume trade between the US and Europe is in balance, and the US Fed lowers American interest rates:

1. Demand for euros will increase due to the greater returns on European investments. This causes the euro to appreciate against the dollar. (Top graph)
2. The stronger euro leads Europeans to demand more American goods. *America's current account balance moves towards surplus and Europe towards deficit.*

3. Over time, the greater demand for American goods will cause demand for dollars to rise and the dollar to appreciate against the euro. (Bottom graph)
4. As the dollar appreciates, European consumers will begin demanding fewer US goods, and Americans more European goods.

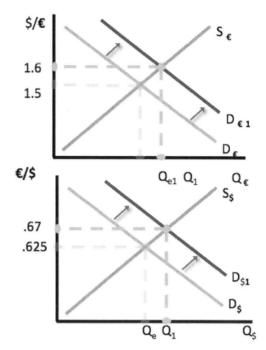

The result of the changing exchange rates is balanced trade over time between the US and Europe!

Consequences of Current Account Deficits
A deficit in the balance of trade between a nation and all others can have some negative short-run and long-run consequences on the nation's economy. Most notably, a trade deficit means a lower level of aggregate demand for the nation.

Assume the country seen here had been producing at its full employment level, but then experienced an increase in its current account deficit:

- Domestic consumption of foreign goods increased, or foreign consumption of domestic goods decreased. Either way, net exports, a component of AD, decreased.
- AD fell and the economy went from achieving full employment into a demand-deficient recession
- Output fell from Yfe to Y2.
- There is deflation in the economy as the average price level falls to P2.

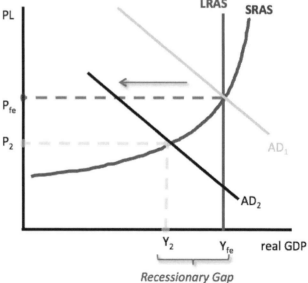

If the current account deficit is not reduced, the economy may experience a decrease in its LRAS as firms reduce investment due expected deflation.

Besides the impact on domestic employment and aggregate demand, the following consequences may result for a nation experiencing a persistent deficit in its current account.

Consequences of a persistent current account deficit	
Depreciation of the currency	A primary determinant of exchange rates is the demand for exports and imports If domestic consumers demand more imports than foreigners demand of the home country's exports, then the value of the domestic currency will fall relative to foreign currencies A weaker currency makes imported raw materials more expensive and can contribute to cost push inflation
Increased foreign ownership of domestic assets	Since current and capital accounts must be in balance, a deficit in the current account means a country likely has a surplus in its capital account. This means foreigners own more of the home country's assets (factories, land, government debt, company shares, etc...) than domestic investors own of foreign assets. Such foreign ownership of domestic assets may pose a threat to the economic sovereignty (freedom) of the deficit country
Higher interest rates	In order to offset the inflationary effects of a weak currency, a country's central bank may try to strengthen the currency by raising interest rates to attract foreign capital to the country. A higher interest rate will negatively effect domestic investment by firms, slowing growth in the nation's capital stock over time.
Increased indebtedness	A current account deficit is offset by a financial account surplus. One of the domestic assets foreign investors will demand is government bonds. Increased selling of bonds by the government to foreign investors increases the amount of national debt held by foreigners. When a government has large amounts of foreign held debt, it must pay interest on that debt, meaning taxpayer money is being paid to foreigners, reducing the government's ability to spend as much on domestic projects like infrastructure, education and health care.

Current Account Deficits and the Exchange Rate

A nation with persistent deficits in its current account should, under a floating exchange rate system, experience a depreciation of its currency on the forex market

Assume the United States if experiencing a large trade deficit with Great Britain

- Americans are spending more on British goods than Brits are on American goods.
- The supply of dollars in Britain is growing faster than the demand for dollars.
- As a result, dollars become less scarce in the forex market, and the value of the dollar falls from 0.65

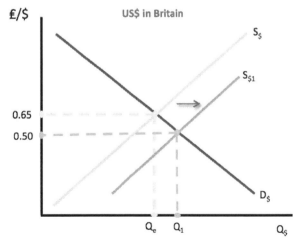

British pounds to 0.50 pounds.

Under a floating exchange rate system, imbalances in the current account should be self-corrected!

- The weaker dollar shown here will make US exports more attractive to British consumers
- Over time, the US current account deficit should be eliminated as US goods begin selling in Britain again

Methods to Correct a Current Account Deficit

The government or central bank of a nation experiencing a persistent current account deficit may choose to intervene to avoid the negative consequences of the deficit on the nation's economy.

Methods for correcting a current account deficit	
Exchange rate devaluation	By intervening in the foreign exchange market a government or central bank can try and *devalue* the country's currency. Trading its own currency for foreign currencies will increase the currency's supply, causing it to depreciate. Greater demand for other countries' currencies will cause them to appreciate. These changes should increase the country's net exports. For this to work, the *Marshall Lerner Condition must be met.*
Expansionary monetary policy	Expansionary monetary policies would lower the country's interest rates and lead to an outflow of capital in the financial account, depreciating the currency and reducing a trade deficit
The use of protectionism	New tariffs or quotas will raise the cost of imported goods and allow domestic producers to sell their products at a higher price at home. Subsidies for domestic producers reduce domestic costs of production and therefore reduce the price of domestic goods, making imports less attractive
Contractionary demand-side policy	An increase in taxes or a decrease in government spending will reduce aggregate demand and the average price level, reducing national income and spending on imports. The lower price level will make exports more attractive to foreigners, bringing the current account into balance.

The Marshall Lerner Condition

Whether or not a depreciation of a nation's currency will cause its current account to move towards deficit depends on the *price elasticity of demand* for exports and imports.

The Marshall Lerner Condition (MLC): If the combined PEDs for exports and imports are *greater than one (e.g. elastic)* then a depreciation of the currency will cause the current account balance to move towards surplus.

- If the MLC is met, then a country can successfully reduce a current account deficit by devaluing its currency.
- If the MLC is NOT met, then currency devaluation will actually worsen a current account deficit.

Rationale: Consumers must be *relatively responsive* to the changing prices of imports and exports in order for a currency devaluation to be effective. For instance,

- If demand for a nation's exports is highly *inelastic*, then their cheaper prices abroad (following a devaluation of the currency), will actually result in foreigners spending *less* on the nation's goods (since they will have to give up less of their own currency to buy them).
- If demand for imports is highly *inelastic*, then a devaluation result in domestic consumers actually spending *more* on imports, since they are now more expensive and the quantities demanded have not decreased by much.
- In this situation, the MLC is NOT met and a weaker currency will lead to a larger trade deficit.

The J Curve

Recall from microeconomics that consumers tend to be *more responsive* to price changes as time passes following the change in price. Based on this knowledge, we can predict what will happen to a nation's current account balance *over time* following a depreciation of its currency.

Assume the country to the right was experiencing a current account deficit:

- The central bank decides to devalue the currency by lowering interest rates and increasing its supply on forex markets.
- In the first several weeks following the devaluation, consumers at home and abroad are relatively *unresponsive* to the country's now higher priced imports

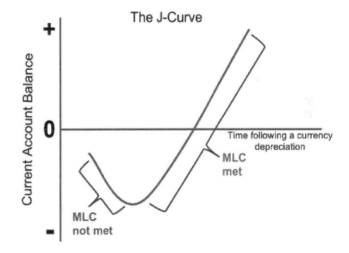

and lower priced exports. The MLC is not met, so the current account deficit actually *worsens.*

- However, after a couple of months, consumers at home and abroad have begun to respond to the country's cheaper exports and the more expensive imports from abroad. The MLC is now met and the current account begins to move towards surplus.

Conclusion: Currency devaluations will be ineffective at correcting current account deficits in the short-run. But over time, a weaker currency will likely move a nation's current account towards surplus as consumers become more responsive to the higher prices of imports and the lower prices of exports!

Consequences of Current Account Surpluses

A current account surplus occurs when a nation's exports are greater than its imports over a period of time. A persistent current account surplus has some positive effects for a nation, but also some negative ones.

Consequences of persistent current account surpluses	
Appreciation of the currency	Since a current account surplus means the country is exporting more than it is importing, foreigners are demanding more of the surplus nation's currency, putting upward pressure on the value of the exchange rate. An appreciating currency will harm producers in the export sector and could reduce domestic employment
Increased ownership of foreign assets	A surplus in the current account is usually offset by a deficit in the financial account. Domestic investors will increase their ownership of foreign assets (stocks, government debt, real estate and factories), meaning there is a net outflow of capital from the country
Reduced levels of domestic consumption	If a nation exports a large proportion of its total output, there is less stuff left over for domestic households to consume While a current account surplus may be good for employment, it is often bad for domestic consumption, since the money earned from exported goods and services is not entirely spent on imports
Possibility of increased protectionism	Foreign governments unhappy with the trade imbalance with the surplus nation may threaten to impose protectionist measures on the exporting nation's goods. Such measures will undermine the surplus nation's comparative advantage and reduce employment and output

Current Account Surpluses and the Exchange Rate

A nation with persistent surpluses in its current account should, under a floating exchange rate system, experience an appreciation of its currency on the forex market

Assume Great Britain is experiencing a persistent current account surplus with the US.

- The high level of demand for British goods in the US will cause demand for British pounds to increase over time.
- Because British consumers are not buying as many US goods, the supply of British pounds will NOT keep up with demand.

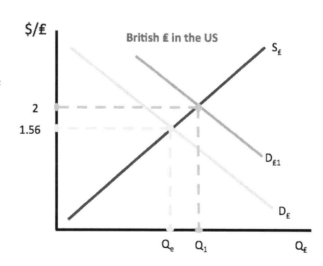

- These effects cause the British pound to appreciate against the dollar.

Assuming the Marshall Lerner Condition is met, this appreciation of the British Pound will lead to a reduction of the current account surplus as higher priced British goods become less attractive to US consumers and cheaper American goods more attractive to British consumers!

Macroeconomics Glossary

Absolute advantage	When a country or individual has can produce a good using fewer resources than another country or individual
Absolute poverty	The state of people who live on less than $1.25 per day (purchasing power parity), as defined by the World Bank. Generally, such individual are unable to afford the basic necessities of life: food, shelter, education, health, etc.
Aggregate Demand	A schedule or curve which shows the total demand for the goods and services of a nation at a range of price levels and at a given period of time.
Aggregate demand and Aggregate supply Model	A model of a nation's economy which shows the average price level and the level of national output resulting from the interaction of the total demand for the nation's output and the total supply of the nation's output. There are different interpretations of the model based Keynesian Economic Theory and Classical Economic Theory.
Aggregate Supply	The total amount of goods and services that all the firms in all the industries in a country will produce at various price levels in a given period of time.
Appreciation	An increase in the value of one currency relative to another, resulting from an increase in demand for or a decrease in supply of the currency on the foreign exchange market.
Balance of Payments	Measures all the monetary exchanges between one nation and all other nations. Includes the current account and the capital account.
Bond	A certificate of debt issued by a company or a government to an investor.
Budget deficit	When a government spends more than it collects in tax revenues.
Business Cycle	A model showing the short run periods of contraction and expansion in output, resulting from fluctuations in the level of aggregate demand, experienced by an economy over a period of time.
Capital	Human-made resources (machinery and equipment) used to produce goods and services; goods that do not directly satisfy human wants.
Capital Flight	When the scarce capital available to a less developed country leaves for the safety and security of a more developed economy. Financial capital flight occurs when savers prefer to put their money in foreign banks to domestic banks, reducing the supply of loanable funds in a poor county. Human capital flight is also known as "brain drain" when the skilled workers in a poor country prefer to seek work in a richer country, reducing the production possibilities of the less developed

	country.
Ceteris paribus	"All else equal"; used as a reminder that all variables other than the ones being studied are assumed to be constant.
Choice	In economics, decisions must be made between the various alternative uses for society's scarce resources. Every choice involves an opportunity cost.
Circular flow	A model of the economy that shows the interconnectedness of businesses, households, government, banks and the foreign sectors in resource markets and product markets. Money flows in a circular direction, and goods, services and resources flow in the opposite direction.
Classical economic theory	The 'supply-side' view that an economy will self-correct from periods of economic shock if left alone. Also known as laissez faire.
Command Economy	An economic system in which resources are allocated through central planning, usually by the state or central government.
Commodity	A good widely demanded (often globally) and supplied by many sellers, usually without much product differentiation between sellers. Commodities are standardized products. The price of commodities is determined by the market as a whole, often in the global market, not by any individual producer or group of producers. Often traded on national or international commodities markets. Examples include oil, wheat, corn, coffee, copper, cotton, tin, rice, gold, and other primary goods.
Common market	A free trade agreement in with all the characteristics of a customs union, but in which the member nations also remove all barriers to the flow of factors of production between them. Labor and capital can move between member states without any government interference.
Comparative advantage	When an individual, a firm or a nation is able to produce a particular product at a lower opportunity cost than another individual, firm or nation. Forms the basis on which nations trade with one another.
Consumer Price Index (CPI)	An index which measures the price of a fixed market basked of consumer goods bought by a typical consumer. Used to calculate the inflation rate in a nation.
Consumption	A component of a nation's aggregate demand, measures the total spending by domestic households on domestically produced goods and services.
Contractionary fiscal policy	A demand-side policy whereby government increases taxes or decreases it expenditures in order to reduce aggregate demand. Could be used in a period of high inflation to bring the inflation rate down.
Contractionary	Contractionary monetary policy: A demand-side policy whereby the

monetary policy	central bank reduces the supply of money, increasing interest rates and reducing aggregate demand. Could be used to bring down high inflation rates.
Cost-push inflation	An increase in the average price level resulting from a decrease in aggregate supply (from higher wage rates and raw material prices) and accompanied by a decrease in real output and employment.
Crowding-out effect	The rise in interest rates and the resulting decrease in investment spending in the economy caused by increased borrowing in the loanable funds market by the government.
Current account	Measures the balance of trade in goods and services and the flow of income between one nation and all other nations. It also records monetary gifts or grants that flow into our out of a country.
Current account deficit	When the value of a nation's imports from abroad exceeds the value of the exports from that nation to the rest of the world. Also called a trade deficit.
Current account surplus	When the value of a nation's exports to the rest of the world exceeds the value of its imports from the rest of the world. Also called a trade surplus.
Customs union	A free trade agreement under which member nations agree to remove all protectionist measures (tariffs, quotas, etc.) between member states, but maintain common external tariffs on imports from non-member states.
Cyclical unemployment	Caused by a fall in aggregate demand in a nation, thus occurs when a nation is in a recession. Not included in the natural rate of unemployment.
Debt cancellation	See indebtedness. When international lenders from a more economically developed country (MEDC) who are owed money by the government of a less economically developed country (LEDC),usually from loans taken out by corrupt governments in the past, forgive the debt they are owed. Allows for the limited tax revenues collected by the developing country's government to be used to provide public goods and services (such as infrastructure, education and health care) which contribute to the poor country's economic development.
Deflation	A decrease in the average price level of a nation's output over time.
Deflationary gap	Also called the recessionary gap. The difference between the equilibrium level of national output in a nation and the full employment level of output when a nation is in a demand-deficient recession. Called "deflationary gap" because the fall in AD that caused it likely caused some deflation in the economy as well.
Demand	A schedule or curve showing the quantities of a particular good demanded at a range of price in a particular period of time.

Demand deposit (Checkable deposit)	Money held by households in a commercial bank against which checks may be written (or debit cards can be used).
Demand side policies	Actions implemented by the government or the central bank aimed at either increasing (expansionary) or decreasing (contractionary) aggregate demand to promote the achievement of several macroeconomic objectives.
Demand-pull inflation	An increase in the average price level resulting from an increase in AD without a corresponding increase in AS.
Depreciation	A decrease in the value of one currency relative to another, resulting from a decrease in demand for or an increase in the supply of the currency on the forex market.
Deterioration in terms of trade	Occurs when the price of a nation's exports decreases relative to the price of its imports. May lead to an improvement in the current account balance if demand for imports is elastic relative to export demand, or a worsening in the current account balance if import demand is relatively inelastic.
Devaluation	When a government or a central bank intervenes in the market for its own currency to weaken it relative to another currency or currencies. May be achieved through measures such as reducing domestic interest rates, selling the currency on foreign exchange markets, or imposing foreign exchange controls that limit the amount of foreign investment in the country, reducing demand for the currency abroad.
Direct taxation	Taxes placed on income.
Discount rate	One of the three tools of monetary policy, it is the interest rate which the FED charges on the loans they make to commercial banks.
Diversification	Producing a variety of different goods as a strategy to protect a nation from the unforeseen demand shocks, which often disrupt the economic growth and development of certain developing nations, which are over-dependent on the production of single commodity (e.g. oil, coffee, diamonds, bananas).
Dumping	The practice of producers in one nation selling their output at a price lower than their costs of production in another nation. Considered a justification for protectionism by the World Trade Organization.
Economic Development	Improvements in standards of living of a nation measured by income, education and health. The Human Development Index is a widely used indicator of the levels of development of various nations.
Economic growth	An increase in the output of goods and services in a nation between two periods of time.

Economic resources	Land, labor, capital, and entrepreneurial ability which are used in the production of goods and services. They are economic resources because they are scarce (limited in supply and desired). Also called the factors of production.
Equity	The idea of "fairness" in economics.
Excess reserves	The amount by which a bank's actual reserves exceeds its required reserves. The amount of excess reserves in the banking system determines equilibrium interest rate.
Exchange rate	The price of one currency in terms expressed in terms of another currency, determined in the forex market.
Expectations	Refers to the assumptions individual households and firms hold about future economic conditions. Current decisions are often made based on expectations of the future.
Expenditure-reducing policies	Measures a government may undertake to improve an imbalance in the current account. If a nation has a large current account deficit, a decrease in spending on imports moves the current account towards surplus. Reducing overall spending in the economy (including on imports) by raising income taxes and reducing government spending (contractionary fiscal policies) can improve the trade balance.
Expenditure-switching policies	Measures undertaken by a government to reduce a deficit in the country's current account balance. Involve increased barriers to trade (tariffs, quotas or protectionist subsidies) aimed at switching the expenditures of domestic consumers from imported goods and services to domestically produced goods and services.
Expenditures approach to GDP	The method for measuring the value of a nation's output which adds all the expenditures made for final goods and services to measure the GDP (the alternative is to add up incomes – the income approach), Equals Consumption +Investment +Government spending + Net Exports
Export-led Growth	A strategy for economic growth and development focused on producing exports to sell to consumers in more developed countries. Also known as "outward-oriented" growth strategy.
Exports	The spending by foreigners on domestically produced goods and services. Counts as an injection into a nation's circular flow of income.
Factors of Production	Include the human and natural resource needed to produce any good or service: Land, labor, capital and entrepreneurship
Fair Trade	A trade scheme which promotes better working and living conditions among the producers of primary commodities such as bananas and coffee in less developed countries. Attempts to assure that a larger percentage of the final sale price of such commodities makes it back to those who produced them.

Federal Funds Rate	The interest rate banks charge one another on overnight loans made out of their excess reserves. The FFR is the interest rate targeted by the Fed through its open market operations.
Financial account	Measures the flow of funds for investment in real assets (such as factories or office building) or financial assets (such as stocks and bonds) between a nation and the rest of the world.
Fiscal policy	Fiscal policy: Changes in government spending and tax collections implemented by government with the aim of either increasing or decreasing aggregate demand to achieve the macroeconomic objectives of full employment and price level stability.
Floating exchange rate	When a currency's price relative to other currencies is determined by the free interaction of supply and demand in international forex markets.
Foreign Direct Investment (FDI)	Investment in factors of production abroad by multi-national corporations.
Foreign exchange market	The market in which international buyers and sellers exchange foreign currencies for one another to buy and sell goods, services, and assets from various countries. It is where a currency's exchange rate relative to other currencies is determined.
Fractional reserve banking	A system in which banks hold only a fraction of their total deposits in reserve and lend out any excess reserves to borrowers. The proportion of total deposits banks must hold in reserve depends on the required reserve ratio.
Free market economy	An economic system in which resources are allocated purely by the forces of demand, supply and the price mechanism. The government has no influence over what is produced, how it is produced and for whom.
Free Trade	The exchange of goods and services between different countries undertaken without any government intervention.
Free Trade Agreement	An agreement between two or more nations to reduce or eliminate barriers to trade across member states. Meant to achieve a more efficient allocation of resources between nations and a larger market for member nation's exports, as well as a larger variety of goods for domestic consumers to enjoy.
Free trade area	An agreement between nations to reduce or remove tariffs and quotas on all goods traded between the member states. Nations can maintain their own external barriers to trade, thus this is a lower level of economic integration than a customs union, but it represents a higher level of integration than a preferential trade area.
Frictional unemployment	When workers are voluntarily moving between jobs, or when recent college graduates are looking for their first job. Considered part of the

natural rate of unemployment.

Full employment	When an economy is producing at a level of output at which almost all the nation's resources are employed. The unemployment rate at this level of output equals the natural rate of unemployment, and includes only frictional and structural unemployment.
GDP (expenditure approach)	Consumption + Investment + Government spending + Net Exports: Measures the total spending on goods and services produced in a nation in a year.
GDP (income approach)	Wages + Interest + Rent + Profit: Measures the total income earned by a nation's households from the production of goods and services in a year.
GDP (per capita)	The total value of a nation's output divided by the number of people in the country. Gives a more accurate measure of the level of income of a nation than the GDP alone.
GDP Deflator	The price index which takes into account all final goods and services produces in a nation. Used to adjust the nominal GDP into real GDP. Nominal GDP divided by this gives you the real GDP.
GDP growth rate	Measures the percentage change in a nation's GDP between one year and an earlier year. Equals Year 2's GDP minus Year 1's GDP, divided by year 1's GDP times 100. For example: If in 2011 GDP = 120 billion, and in 2010 it equaled 100 billion. The GDP growth rate = (120-100)/100 = 0.2 x 100 = 20%
Gini Coefficient	A numerical measure of the level of income inequality in a nation. Measures the ratio of the area between the line of equality (the 45 degree line) and a nation's Lorenz Curve to the total area below the line of equality. The closer the coefficient is to one, the more unequal a nation's income distribution. The closer to zero, the more equal the nation's income is distributed.
Globalization	The emerging inter-connectedness of the world's national economies and cultures
Government spending	A component of a nation's GDP, consisting of all expenditures made by a nation's government in a year on public goods, services and infrastructure in a nation.
Gross Domestic Product (GDP)	The total market value of all final goods and services produced during a given time period within a country's borders. Equal to the total income of the nation's households or the total expenditures on the nation's output.
Human capital	The value of labor created through education, training, knowledge and health. An important determinant of aggregate supply and the level of economic growth in a nation.

Human Development Index (HDI)	A measure of the standards of living, used to rank countries based on their level of human development. It takes into account three primary variables: the level of GDP per capita, (as an indication of income levels), literacy (as an indication of education levels), and life expectancy (as an indication of levels of health). Countries are placed into one of four categories based on their HDI ranking: "very high human development", "high human development", "medium human development" and "low human development".
Hyperinflation	A rapid and accelerating increase in the average price level in a nation, usually caused by monetary expansion (increases in the money supply without corresponding increases in national output)
Import substitution	A strategy for economic growth and development focused on producing goods for the domestic market to replace the goods that consumers may have bought from foreign firms previously. Requires the use of protectionism to keep foreign imports out of the domestic market. Also known as "inward-oriented growth strategy".
Imports	Spending on goods and services produced in foreign nations. Counts as a leakage from a nation's circular flow of income.
Improvement in terms of trade	When the price of a nation's exports rises relative to the price of its imports. May result in an improvement in the current account balance if demand for the country's exports is inelastic relative to its import demand, or a worsening in the current account balance if export demand is elastic relative to import demand.
Income	The money earned by households for providing their resources (land, labor and capital) to firms in the resource market. Incomes include wages, interest, rent and profit.
Indebtedness	When a country owes money to lenders, generally foreigners, requiring a large percentage of any tax revenues collected to go towards servicing the national debt. Presents an obstacle to economic development since poor countries find they have little money left over for the provision of public goods to citizens.
Infant Industry	An industry that is emerging in a less developed country, but which has not achieved the economies of scale and other efficiencies that allow it to compete with larger producers in more developed countries. Sometimes used as a justification for protectionist policies.
Inflation	A rise in the average level of prices in the economy over time, measured by the percentage change in the Consumer Price Index (CPI).
Inflation rate	The percentage change in the CPI from one period to the next. Knowing the consumer price index for two periods of time, inflation can be measures: [(CPI2 - CPI1)/CPI1] x 100. For example. If the CPI in 2011 = 156 and the CPI in 2010 = 150, then the inflation rate equals (156 – 150)/150 = 0.04 x 100 = 4%. The inflation rate was 4% between

2010 and 2011.

Inflationary gap	The difference between a nation's equilibrium level of output and its full employment level of output when the nation is over-heating (producing beyond its full employment level).
Inflationary spiral	The rapid increase in average price level resulting from demand pull inflation leading to higher wages, causing cost push inflation.
Infrastructure	The physical assets of a nation which increase the efficiency with which the nation produces its output. Includes all the roads, electricity grids, water and sewage facilities, but also factories, airports, railways, tunnels, bridges schools and hospitals: anything that increases the productivity of labor in the nation.
Interest	The payment for capital in the resource market. Firms pay interest on the money they borrow to acquire capital equipment (technology). Households receive interest for providing their savings to banks, which make the loans to the firms paying interest.
Interest rate	The opportunity cost of money. Either the cost of borrowing money or the cost of spending money. What would be given up by not saving money.
Investment	A component of aggregate demand, it includes all spending on capital equipment, inventories, and technology by firms. This does not include financial investment, which is the purchase of financial assets (stocks and bonds), not included in GDP because they are only purely financial investments.
J-Curve	A graph showing the likely change in a nation's current account balance over time following a depreciation of the nation's currency. Called "J-curve" because in the short-run, the current account is likely to move down, into deficit, but in the long-run (once consumers at home and abroad become more responsive to the weaker currency), net exports will increase and the current account will move towards surplus.
Keynesian Economic Theory	The theory, developed by John Maynard Keynes during the Great Depression, that the government should take an active role in managing the level of aggregate demand in an economy. During recessions, government should run budget deficits (lower taxes and increase government spending) to stimulate AD and move the economy back towards full employment. During inflationary periods, the government should raise taxes and reduce government spending to bring AD back to its full employment level.
Labor	The work undertaken by humans towards the production of goods and services
Land	Includes all natural resources needed to undertake production of goods or services: including soil, timber, minerals, fossil fuels, fresh water,

livestock, fish, etc... "the gifts of nature"

Loanable funds market	The market in which the demand for private investment and the supply of household savings intersect to determine the equilibrium real interest rate. Can be used to illustrate the crowding-out effect of deficit-financed fiscal policy, which causes the supply of funds to become more scarce as households save more money in government bonds.
Long-run (macroeconomics)	The period of time over which the wage rate and price level in a nation are flexible. In the long run, any changes in AD be cancelled out due to the flexibility of wages and prices and an economy will return to its full employment level of output. Sometimes referred to as the flexible wage period.
Long-run aggregate supply	A curve on the aggregate demand and aggregate supply model that is vertical at the nation's full employment level of output. Due to the fact that wages and prices are flexible in the long run, a nation's economy will always return to its full employment level of output following a change in aggregate demand, according to classical economic theory, at least.
Long-run Economic growth	An increase in national output resulting from an increase in aggregate supply. If GDP rises because the nation's resources became more productive or more abundant, then the full employment level of output will increase, indicating that such growth in sustainable, and most likely characterized by low inflation (i.e. stable price levels).
Lorenz Curve	A curve showing the distribution of income within a nation. Shows what percentage of the total income in a nation is earned by each quintile (e.g. the top 20% versus the middle or the bottom 20%)
M1	A component of the money supply including currency and checkable deposits.
M2	A more broadly defined component of the money supply. Equal to M1 plus savings deposits, money market deposits, mutual funds, and small time deposits.
M3	The broadest component of the money supply. Equal to M2 plus large time deposits.
Macroeconomic equilibrium	The level of output at which a nation is producing at any particular period of time. May be below its full employment level (if the economy is in recession) or beyond its full employment level (if the economy is over-heating).
Macroeconomics	The study of entire nations' economies and the interactions between households, firms, government and foreigners.
Managed exchange rate	When a government or central bank takes action to manage or fix the value of its currency relative to another currency on the forex market.

Marginal	Means "additional". An important term in economics, which often focuses on "marginal analysis" meaning we compare the additional cost of an action to the additional benefit it creates.
Marginal analysis	Decision making which involves a comparison of marginal (extra) benefits and marginal costs.
Marginal propensity to consume (MPC)	The proportion of any change in income spent on domestically produced goods and services; equal to the change in consumption divided by the change in disposable income. One divided by 1-MPC determines the size of the Keynesian spending multiplier.
Marginal propensity to save (MPS)	The proportion of any change in income that is saved; equal to the change in savings divided by the change in disposable income. One divided by the MPS determines the size of the Keynesian spending multiplier.
Market	A place where buyers and sellers meat to engage in mutual trade. Prices are set by the interaction of demand and supply in a market.
Market system	Market economic system: A system of resource allocation in which buyers and sellers meet in markets to determine the price and quantity of goods, services and productive resources.
Marshall-Lerner Condition	Determines how depreciation in a currency's exchange rate will affect the nation's current account balance. If the combined price elasticities of demand for exports and imports is greater than one (elastic), then a depreciation of the currency will move the current account towards surplus. But if demand for exports and imports is inelastic, a weaker currency will move the current account towards deficit.
Micro-credit	The extension of very small loans (a few hundred dollars or less, typically) to borrowers in less developed countries meant to give small entrepreneurs access to simple capital. Has proven a successful strategy for economic development.
Microeconomics	The study of the interactions between consumers and producers in markets for individual products.
Mixed economy	Most economies today are mixed economies, i.e. sharing characteristics of the free market system but with an active role for government.
Monetarism	The macroeconomic view that the main cause of changes in aggregate output and the price level are fluctuations in the money supply.
Monetary policy	The central bank's manipulation of the supply of money aimed at raising or lowering interest rates to stimulate or contract the level of aggregate demand to promote the macroeconomic objectives of price level stability and full employment.

Money	Any object that can be used to facilitate the exchange of goods and services in a market.
Money demand	The sum of the transaction demand and the asset demand for money. Inversely related to the nominal interest rate. Increases and decreases (shifts to the right or left) with the level of national output.
Money market	The market where the supply of money is set by the central bank, includes the downward sloping money demand curve and a vertical money supply curve. The "price" of money is the nominal interest rate.
Money Multiplier	1/RRR (required reserve ratio). Tells the total amount by which total deposits will increase by in the banking system following an initial change in checkable deposits. For example: an initial injection of $1000 of new money into an economy with a reserve ratio of 0.1 will generate $1000 x (10) = $10,000 in total money.
Money supply	The vertical curve representing the total supply of reserves in a nation's banking system. Determined by the monetary policy actions of the central bank. Increases (shifts to the right) lead to lower interest rates and are the result of expansionary monetary policies. Decreases (shifts to the left) lead to higher interest rates and are the result of contractionary monetary policies.
Multiplier effect	The theory that a particular increase in private or government spending (C, I, G, or Xn) in an economy will lead to a larger overall increase in GDP than the initial change in spending, due to the fact that the increase in incomes that result will lead to further increases in private spending throughout the economy. The size of the multiplier effect depends on the spending multiplier.
National economy	A macroeconomic term referring to the sum of the economic activity undertaken by a nation's households and firms in the product and resource market in a year. The circular flow model offers a graphical representation, showing the flow of money and resources in a nation. The aggregate demand / aggregate supply model is another graphical representation, showing the average price level, the level of output and the level of total demand and supply for a nation's output.
National income	Another term for the GDP of a nation. Measures the total income earned by households in the resources market for their provision of labor, land, capital and entrepreneurship to the nation's producers.
National output	Another term for the GDP of a nation. Measures the value of all the finished goods and services produced in the nation in a year.
Natural rate of unemployment	The level of unemployment that prevails in an economy that is producing at its full employment level of output. Includes structural and frictional unemployment.
Net Export effect	The fall in net exports resulting from a deficit-financed fiscal stimulus. When a government deficit spends, it will drive up domestic interest

rates (see crowding-out effect), causing the country's currency to appreciate on the foreign exchange market. This reduces demand for the country's exports, reducing the expansionary effect of the deficit financed government spending.

Net exports	A component of aggregate demand. Equals the income earned from the sale of exports to the rest of the world minus expenditures by domestic consumers on imports.
Nominal GDP	The quantity of various goods produced in a nation times their current prices, added together. Can increase either as a result of an increase in real output or an increase in the price level.
Nominal interest rate	The price of money. If an individual wishes to borrow money, this determines the percentage they must pay back to the lender in addition to the amount borrowed. Also, it represents the return earned (as a percentage) by a saver for keeping his or her money in the bank. Does not reflect the effect of inflation on borrowers and savers (see real interest rate).
Normative statement	A normative statement is one based on opinion. For example, "the government should lower income taxes".
Official reserves	Foreign currencies held by a nation's central bank, resulting from accumulations in the current account and the financial account in the nation's balance of payments. To balance the two accounts in the balance of payments, a country's official foreign exchange reserves measures the net effect of all the money flows from the other accounts.
Open market operations	The central bank's buying and selling of government bonds on the open market from commercial banks and the public. Aimed at increasing or decreasing the level of reserves in the banking system and thereby affecting the interest rate and the level of aggregate demand. Selling bonds takes money out of circulation, reducing the supply of money and raising the interest rate (contractionary monetary policy). The Fed's buying of bonds increases the amount of money in circulation, increasing the money supply and reducing interest rates (expansionary monetary policy).
Opportunity cost	What must be given up to have anything else. Not necessarily monetary costs, rather include what you could do with the resources you use to undertake any activity or exchange.
Phillips Curve	A downward sloping curve showing the short run tradeoff between the level of inflation and the level of unemployment in a nation. As the inflation rate increases in the short-run, the unemployment rate decreases, and as unemployment increases, inflation decreases. There is also a long-run curve which is vertical at the natural rate of unemployment showing that in the long run there is no trade off between the price level and the level of unemployment in an economy.
Positive statement	A claim which can be proven with facts. For example, "The

unemployment rate has risen for two consecutive quarters."

Potential Output	How much a nation can produce if all of its resources (land, labor and capital) are operating at their full capacity and at full efficiency. Contrasts with full employment output, which a nation achieves when most of its resources are employed towards production, but there exist some degree of unemployment (the natural rate of unemployment).
Preferential trade agreement	A free trade agreement in which member states agree to remove protectionist measures on certain goods or services traded between them. The lowest level of economic integration, since only particular goods are included in the agreement.
Private sector	Refers to the activities undertaken by the private households and firms in an economy. "Private sector spending" includes household consumption and investment by private, non-government-owned firms.
Product market	The market in a nation's circular flow of income in which households demand goods and services, which firms provide. Households make purchases, providing revenue for firms, which they in turn use to acquire resources from households in the resource market.
Production possibilities curve	A graph that shows the various combinations of output that the economy can possibly produce given the available factors of production and the available production technology.
Productivity	The output per unit of input of a resource. An important determinant of the level of aggregate supply in a nation. Will increase as a result of better or more capital, education and health, all which add to the human capital of a nation.
Progressive tax	A tax on income that increases in percentage as an individual's income increases. For example, when an individual earning $50,000 pays 15% and an individual earning $100,000 pays 25% in tax.
Proportional tax	A tax that places a proportionally identical burden on every individual regardless of their income. For example an income tax that requires everyone to pay 10% regardless of their income. A rich household will pay more than a lower income household, but the percentage of income paid in tax is identical.
Protectionism	Protectionism: The use of tariffs, quotas or subsidies to give domestic producers a competitive advantage over foreign producers. Meant to protect domestic production and employment from foreign competition.
Public sector	Refers to the activities undertaken by the government or the state. "Public sector investment" generally refers to government spending on infrastructure.
Quantity theory of money	MV = PY – The quantity of money in a nation (Q) times the velocity of money (V) equals the average price level (P) times the level of output). The monetarist's view that explains how changes in the money supply

will affect the price level assuming the velocity of money and the level of output are fixed.

Quota	A physical limit on the quantity of a good produced in a foreign country allowed to be imported. Meant to restrict imports, allowing domestic producers to sell a greater quantity on the domestic market.
Rational expectations theory	The idea that business firms and households expect monetary and fiscal policies to have certain effects on the economy and take, in pursuit of their own self-interests, actions which make these policies ineffective.
Real GDP	Measures the value of a nation's output in a period of time adjusted for any inflation or deflation the economy has experienced. Equals the nominal GDP divided by the GDP deflator price index.
Real interest rate	Represents the opportunity cost of borrowing money or the return earned on savings, adjusted for the rate of inflation in the economy. Equals the nominal interest rate minus the inflation rate.
Recession	A decrease in the total output of goods and services in a nation between two periods of time. Could be caused by a decrease in aggregate demand or in aggregate supply.
Recessionary gap	The difference between an economy's equilibrium level of output and its full employment level of output when an economy is in recession.
Regressive tax	A tax that places a smaller burden on the incomes of the rich than it does the poor. For example a sales tax that adds $1000 to the price of a product (say a 10% tax on a $10,000 car) places a larger burden on someone earning $50,000 (2% of his income) than someone earning $100,000 (1% of his income). A sales tax is therefore a regressive tax.
Relative poverty	The state of earning an income that puts one in the lowest income level within his or her country. Unlike absolute poverty, it exists everywhere, since within even the richest nations a proportion of the population earns relatively less than the top income earners.
Rent	The price of land resources. Rent must be paid by producers, either as an explicit cost or as an opportunity cost for those who own the land resources employed in production.
Required reserves	The proportion of a bank's total deposits it is required to keep in reserve with the central bank. Determined by the required reserve ratio.
Resource market	The market in a nation's circular flow in which households provide firms with the factors of production (land, labor and capital) in exchange for money incomes (rent, wages and interest). Firms are the buyers, households are the sellers in the resource market.
Revaluation	When a government or central bank intervenes in the market for its own currency on foreign exchange market to raise its value relative to

another currency or currencies. Measures may include raising domestic interest rates, purchasing the currency using foreign exchange reserves, or restricting the outflow of capital for foreign investment (exchange controls).

Scarcity

When something is both desired and limited in supply. All resources (land, labor and capital) are limited in supply, yet desired for their use in the production of goods and services.

Seasonal unemployment

A type of frictional unemployment in which a worker is in between jobs that may only be only available during certain seasons. For example a ski instructor who guides rafting trips in the summer will be seasonally unemployed in the spring and fall.

Self-correction

The idea that an economy producing at an equilibrium level of output that is below or above its full employment will return on its own to its full employment level if left to its own devices. Requires flexible wages and prices, and therefore is only likely to happen in the long-run (macroeconomics).

Services

The non-physical output of firms meant for consumption in a product market. Services are "non-tangible" goods, such as taxi rides, accounting, doctor visits, teaching, and other products that can be bought and sold, but not physically consumed.

Short run aggregate supply

An upward sloping curve, relatively flat below the full employment level of output, and relatively steep beyond the full employment level, showing the amount of output a nation's producers will supply at a range of price levels in a particular period of time. The curve's shape reflects the fact that output cannot grow beyond the full employment level due to the limited factors of production available in the economy, but when aggregate demand falls output will decline due to the inflexibility of wages in the short run.

Short-run

(In macroeconomics): The period of time over which wages and prices are relatively inflexible. A fall in aggregate demand will lead to unemployment and recession in the short-run. Due to the inability of the nation's producers to reduce wages paid to worker, they must lay workers off to reduce costs as demand falls.

Short-run Economic growth

Results from an increase in aggregate demand without a corresponding increase in aggregate supply. GDP increases because demand increased. Considered short-run because without increases in the productive capacity of the nation's resources, such growth will not be sustainable and an economy will return to its full-employment level of national output.

Social science

One of the fields of study that examine humans' social interactions and institutions. Includes economics, sociology, psychology, archaeology, political science, linguistics, etc.

Specialization

The practice of allocating an individual's, an organization's or a nation's resources towards the production of a good or a category of goods for which it has a relatively low opportunity cost. Improves the overall allocation of resources and allows individuals and, with trade, allows individuals or nations to consume beyond what they would be able to produce on their own.

Speculation	The buying and selling of currencies or other assets based on the expectation of future changes in exchange rates or prices. Speculation is a major determinant of the exchange rate of the world's currencies.
Spending multiplier	1/(1-MPC), or 1/MPS, where MPC is the marginal propensity to consume and MPS is the marginal propensity to save. It tells you how much total spending an initial injection of spending in the economy will generate. For example, if the MPC = .8 and the government spends $100 million, then the total increase in spending in the economy = $100 x 5 = $500 million.
Stagflation	A macroeconomic situation in which both inflation and unemployment increase. Caused by a negative supply shock.
Sticky-wages	The short run aggregate supply curve is sometimes referred to as the "inflexible wage and price model", because workers' wage demands take time to adjust to changes in the overall price level; therefore, in the short run an economy may produce well below or beyond its full employment level of output. Explains why short run aggregate supply is horizontal below full employment and nearly vertical beyond full employment.
Structural unemployment	Caused by changes in the structure of demand for goods and in technology; workers who are unemployed because their skills do not match what is in demand by producers in the economy.
Subsidy	Payments made from the government to individuals or firms for the production or consumption of particular goods or services. Subsidies reduce the cost of production or increase the benefit of consumption, and therefore lead to a greater equilibrium quantity in the market for the subsidized good.
Supply shock	Anything that leads to a sudden, unexpected change in aggregate supply. Can be negative (decreases AS) or positive (increases AS). May include a change in energy prices, wages, business taxes, or may result from a natural disaster or a new discovery of important resources.
Sustainability	The ability to endure over time. Sustainable growth requires that resources are used at a rate at which they are able to replenish themselves and the environment is not despoiled in the process of production.
Tariff	Taxes placed on goods imported from other countries. Meant to protect domestic producers from foreign competition.

Tax	A payment made by an individual or a firm to the government, usually levied on income, property or the consumption of goods and services. Taxes are a leakage from the circular flow of income, but they provide government with the money they use to provide government services and public goods.
Tax multiplier	-MPC/MPS, where MPC is the marginal propensity to consume and MPS is the marginal propensity to save. It tells you how much total spending will result from an initial change in the level of taxation. It is negative because when taxes decrease, spending increases, and vice versa. The tax multiplier will always be smaller than the spending multiplier.
Terms of Trade	The ratio of an index of a nation's export prices to its import prices. An improvement in the terms of trade means export prices have risen relative to import prices. A worsening means import prices have risen relative to export prices.
The Basic Economic Questions	What should be produced? How should it be produced? and, "For whom should production take place?" Any economic system, either centrally planned or free market, must address these questions.
Trade creation	When a free trade agreement leads to an increase in efficiency as goods that previously were produced in a high-cost country are now produced in a lower-cost country.
Trade deficit	When a country's total spending on imported goods and services exceeds its total revenues from the sale of exports to the rest of the world. Another term for current account deficit in the balance of payments.
Trade diversion	When a free trade agreement diverts trade from a low-cost that is not involved in the agreement country to a higher cost country that is involved. If trade diversion occurs, a free trade agreement may lead to an overall loss of efficiency in resource allocation in the world.
Trade surplus	When a country's sale of exports exceeds its spending on imports. Another term for a current account surplus in the balance of payments.
Transfer payments	Payments from the government to one group of individuals using tax money raised from taxes on another group of individuals. Meant to reallocate income in an economy, often times from the rich to the poor, but also from households to firms (in the case of subsidies for certain industries).
Under-employment	When a worker is employed in a part-time job but wishes to be working full time. Or when a worker is employed in a job for which he is vastly over-qualified.
Unemployment	The state of an individual who is of working age, actively seeking work, but unable to find a job.

Unemployment rate	The percentage of the labor force that is actively seeking employment but unable to find a job. Equals the number of unemployed divided by the total labor force times 100.
Velocity of money	A measure of the number of times an average unit of currency will be spent in a nation in a year. Assumed to be constant by the monetarist school of macroeconomic theory. A component of the quantity theory of money.
Voluntary Export Restraints	(VER): Limits on exports agreed on by the government or the producers in one nation meant to help producers of particular products in another nation.
Wage	The payment to labor in the resource market. Wages are the "price of labor"
Wealth	An important determinant of consumption. Refers to the total value of a household's assets minus all its liabilities.
World Bank	An international agency which makes soft loans to less economically developed countries, mostly for infrastructure projects or other investments which improve the physical or the human capital of the developing country.
World Trade Organization (WTO)	An organization aimed at liberalizing trade by facilitating the reduction or elimination of trade barriers between member states.

Printed in Germany
by Amazon Distribution
GmbH, Leipzig